Climate Garden 2085
Handbook for a public experiment

Edited by Juanita Schläpfer-Miller and Manuela Dahinden

PARK BOOKS

Concept
Juanita Schläpfer-Miller and Manuela Dahinden

Graphic Design
Manuela Dahinden and Fabian Leuenberger

Editing
Joe Swann and Ruth Niel

Proofreading
Jennifer Taylor

Lithography, Printing and Binding
DZA Druckerei zu Altenburg GmbH, Thuringia

© 2017 Juanita Schläpfer-Miller, Manuela Dahinden and Park Books AG, Zurich
© for the texts: the authors
© for the photographs on p. 43, 77, 79 (left), 80, 85, 88: Juanita Schläpfer-Miller
© for the photographs on p. 60: Christina Della Giustina
© for the photographs on p. 23: Alan Sonfist courtesy of the artist, Mark Dion courtesy the artist and Tanya Bonakdar Gallery, New York
© for all other photographs: Nina Mann
© 2017, ProLitteris, Zurich for the works by Simon Grab, Marcus Maeder and Janeth Berrettini

Park Books AG
Niederdorfstrasse 54
8001 Zurich
Switzerland
www.park-books.com

All rights reserved; no part of this work may be reproduced or edited using electronic systems, copied, or distributed in any form whatsoever without previous written consent from the publisher.

ISBN 978-3-03860-060-2

Citation
Climate Garden 2085: Handbook for a public experiment.
Juanita Schläpfer-Miller and Manuela Dahinden (eds.)
Park Books, 2017.

Zurich-Basel Plant Science Center
The Zurich-Basel Plant Science Center is a competence center that links and supports the plant science research community of the University of Zurich, ETH Zurich and the University of Basel. Our 700 member scientists research in a wide spectrum of plant-related disciplines – from molecular biology to ecosystem research.

Zurich-Basel Plant Science Center
ETH Zurich, LFW B51
Universitätsstrasse 2
8092 Zurich
Switzerland
www.plantsciences.ch

Paper
RecyStar Polar, recycled paper
(FSC, Blauer Engel, EU Ecolabel)

Foreword

What is the Climate Garden 2085?

Climate change has been communicated as a global concern affecting us all, but there is still a disconnect between scientific information and political and social action – the so called climate paradox. This has been a cause for concern for some time now. The *Climate Garden 2085* came about through a very simple question. Although as a science communicator and artist I understood global climate scenarios, I could not imagine what it meant for me as a citizen of Central Europe. What would the future bring for me and my descendants? What would grow in my garden in twenty years? Or in my daughter's garden when she is a grandmother? I hoped that these personal questions would find resonance with others.

As a counter to the information hurricane in which we live, the slow medium of a garden – a narrative environment for holistic sensory immersion – might be able to tell a local story with global significance. In collaboration with the Botanical Garden of the University of Zurich, the Zurich-Basel Plant Science Center initiated this art-science experiment, and invited the public to personally experience climate scenarios and their possible effect on agricultural plants, as well as on our landscape and forests.

This book simultaneously distills and expands the project. Distills, in that it is a documentation of what was, and expands as an invitation to you, its readers, to take the idea and run with it. The story of plants and a changing climate is both local and global: every community in the world will be affected differently, and with the help of this manual, can create a climate garden and tell its own story, enabling a personal, emotional connection to be made with often abstract global climate scenarios.

Part I of the book consists of six short essays in the emerging field of environmental humanities by plant biologists, art and cultural studies scholars, and ecologists, whose analyses position the *Climate Garden 2085* in its social, cultural and scientific context. Part II is a guide to building your own climate garden, based on our experience here in Zurich. Included in this section we have documented the talks, performances and storytelling of artists and scientists who lent us their considerable talents. The photographer Nina Mann was present throughout the summer, and her poetic images illustrate the essays and document the building process, creating a book which will hopefully take on an artistic life of its own.

This project would not have been possible without the support of all our sponsors, to whom we at the *Climate Garden 2085* are deeply indebted. Thank you for your generosity. We are grateful also for the participation of the thousands of visitors who came and shared with us their personal stories and concerns about climate change.

The exhibition is now on tour and will be installed in the Botanical Garden in Bern, in Winterthur and San Francisco, CA.

Juanita Schläpfer-Miller
Zurich, March 2017

Two climate scenarios were created in greenhouses in the Old Botanical Garden in Zurich and maintained from April to September 2016 at temperatures of +2°C and +4°C above the current average monthly summer temperatures. Half the plants in each greenhouse were given 30% less water. The +2°C scenario simulates conditions that will prevail if are curbed in line with the Paris Agreement of 2015. The +4°C scenario simulates the state of affairs if global warming continues at its present rate – as defined by the scenario, downscaling for northeast Switzerland in 2085 (Meteoschweiz/ETH CH-2011). A new calculation for Switzerland is currently being prepared and will be available in 2018.

Plants that currently flourish in northern Switzerland such as ryegrass, sunflowers, wheat, maize and sugar beet were grown both in the greenhouses and outside, to enable comparison between what we currently grow and eat and what may happen in the future. Visitors were able to participate by taking measurements of drought and heat-stressed plants. Complementing the greenhouses, a program of workshops for families and school groups, art performances, and talks by scientists was provided.

Essays

An art-science experiment to address the climate paradox — 9
Connected to place: Climate change on global and local scales — 15
Botanical time travel to unspectacular climatic futures — 20
An ethical discourse on CO_2 reduction — 25
Hothouse stories: Reading the Climate Garden 2085 — 30
Nature in the city: Do-It-Yourself! — 34
Urban ecology — 39

How to Do-It-Yourself!

How to Do-It-Yourself! — 42
Steps to take — 44
Outside experiment — 46

Events in the garden

Art (tree) trail — 50
Unstable balance — 52
Premonition of farewell — 54
Hide tree at school — 57
Storytelling for young children — 58
you are variations — 60
Cypress — 61
Scots pine — 63
Treetment – a conversation to be performed — 64
Tree (art) trail — 69
Cinema — 70
Citizen science — 73
Workshops — 74
Science talks — 80
Walkshop — 84

Evaluation — 86
Observations of the Climate Garden 2085 experiment — 90

Editors and Photographer — 96
Contributors and Resources — 97
Acknowledegements — 98

An art-science experiment to address the climate paradox

Juanita Schläpfer-Miller

Juanita Schläpfer-Miller is a science communicator and artist currently developing outreach programming at the Zurich-Basel Plant Science Center. Her doctoral work investigated knowledge production in transdisciplinary art and science collaborations. She teaches science communication courses at the ETH Zurich and regularly speaks at conferences on science communication and transdisciplinary research.

The climate paradox refers to the disconnect between what citizens know about climate change and their lack of action. Given the scientific and ethical consensus, why are we not acting? Current discussions in climate change communication focus on the importance of understanding individual and social responses, and how to encourage action. I argue that the current issue is one of representation. What and how we tell stories about climate change, and how these narratives are framed really matters if we want people to care and act. In this essay I will first examine some of the barriers to successful communication, and then present the argument that an art-science public experiment such as the *Climate Garden 2085* is uniquely positioned to contribute to the solution, because it shows climate change as something local and material, illustrates the options that remain despite uncertainty, and provides a platform for social learning.

Several barriers to successful climate change communication have been identified. These include: framing climate as distant in space and time, presenting climate change as a disaster, and the role of uncertainty and dissonance – i.e., the gap between understanding and action – which leads to denial.

One aspect of our collective response I find particularly interesting is our attitude to the future and how we identify with temporal and spatial scales. Climate models are based on a concept of time which organizes the data into a time structure that is precise, but too distant for the immediate timescales on which most people base their decisions.[1] The notion of climate change involves specific concepts about the future: Science, public policy, and communication of climate change all create a 'didactic futurology' that attempts to make us care about the future and invest in it now, even though there is (or appears to be) uncertainty about what may or may not come to pass.[2] The crux of the dislocation between public knowledge and public action lies here: in the argument that the scenarios *may or may not come to pass*. What the Intergovernmental Panel on Climate Change (IPCC) seeks to communicate is that one or other scenario will certainly transpire, based on an established chain of past, and a plausible chain of future events. The question is: Which version will transpire and when? It could be argued, however, that even this level of uncertainty dampens commitment to the future.

In their paper *Human geographies of climate change: Landscape, temporality, and lay knowledges*, Catherine Brace and Hilary Geoghegan (2010) state that climate change "can be observed in relation to landscape but also felt, sensed, apprehended emotionally as part of the fabric of everyday life in which acceptance, denial, resignation and action co-exist as personal and social responses to the local manifestations of a global problem."[3]

The theme of framing climate change as a certainly impending disaster of uncertain magnitude has been taken up by Richard Matthew in *Space, time and scales of human security in climate change* (2013), where he investigates universal versus particular narratives. Matthew refers to *Thick and Thin: Moral Argument at Home and Abroad* (1994), in which Michael Walzer writes that "in moral discourse 'thinness' (i.e. universality) and intensity go together, whereas with 'thickness' comes qualification, compromise, complexity and disagreement."[4] In this scheme a thin, but intense, universal story such as genocide or torture can make an impact on a particular community even if they are not directly affected by it. An example of a thick (complex, controversial), or particular story might be the suspected human health effects caused by a local factory which is the only employer in a small community.

Matthew argues that the dominant climate change narrative attempts to impose a thick universal story on humankind, and that this is the narrative form least likely to succeed in persuading the audience. This has come about because, while the fact of anthropogenic-driven climate change is certain, there are uncertainties and planetary variability as to the extent of its specific effects, due to unpredictable feedback responses from natural and human systems. This is partly because complex ecosystems display non-linear behavior, creating uncertainty in exactly how they will behave in future. So although the climate change story should be both universal and intense, prompting moral outrage and action, it ends up being thick and contested, and hence not finding moral entry points into local dialogue.

It is worth taking a small detour here and looking at how narratives of climate change also include information generated by climate scientists. Representations of the scenarios presented by the IPCC are framed in a particular way and carry a set of cognitive assumptions which do not always meet the needs of their target audiences. An interesting study was recently published by the Institute for Atmospheric and Climate Science (IAC) at ETH Zurich. The authors were interested in whether people really understood a widely circulated graph from the IPCC. Rosmarie McMahon conducted interviews with forty people, including politicians, communication experts and academics, and three climate scientists.[5] The subjects were tested for their understanding of graph schemata and salience, for scientific literacy, and for content knowledge. The IPCC graph[6] in question displays two different types of uncertainty: one rooted in socio-economic scenarios – e.g., energy-saving policies and behaviors – and the other due to unpredictable feedback responses from natural systems.

The study found that *only the climate scientists* understood that the uncertainties in the scenario were due to the unpredictability of humans and not to scientific uncertainty in the models. Non-scientists saw a great deal of uncertainty, but falsely attributed it to the climate models and ignored the scenario uncertainties. This is crucial information to policymakers and communicators of climate change, as this graph is widely shown in the media and is an essential tool in climate discourse.[7] The IAC is currently redesigning the graph to improve its comprehensibility.

Understanding of the facts is certainly important, and communication has for a long time focused on this, but psychologists show that unless this knowledge is coupled with action, cognitive dissonance will occur, in the sense that "Climate cannot be that important since I and others are doing nothing about it."[8] People adjust their beliefs to be consistent with their behavior and also to the behavior of their friends and neighbors in order to avoid social dissonance. So what structures might generate and inform better dialogue and affective behavioral change?

As the human brain privileges experience over analysis, climate change has to be communicated as local and personal. That climatic issues are often presented in analytic formats assumes that people process uncertain information in a logical, analytic manner. Yet psychologists have shown that the human brain uses two different processing systems. The first is intuitive, experiential, affective (emotional), and fast. The second is deliberative, analytic, rational and slow. We constantly make judgments using these systems in parallel, but when they diverge, the first system dominates. In other words, how we feel about something has a stronger influence on how we respond than what we think about that issue. From this insight derives the concrete policy recommendation to translate information about climate change risks into "relatable and concrete personal experiences."[9]

The "work" of art

I would argue that art is uniquely positioned to provide such experiences. This has been described as "the 'work' art can do with respect to socio-ecological transformations."[10] Harriet Hawkins has examined *Bird Yarns*, a collective knitting project in Scotland consisting of a flock of knitted Arctic terns which "land" in various locations in Scotland, provoking dialogue about the disturbance in migration patterns due to climate change. The project has created an international network of knitters sharing patterns, wool and finished birds: "*Bird Yarns* offered knitters – and, in part, the local community – the chance to register a different imaginary of earthly and atmospheric collectivities than one focused on scientific fact."[11] The artwork offers not only a different imaginative experience but also "localizes and materializes climate change," bringing epic narratives to a situation closer to home.[12] This topic is taken up by Emily-Eliza Scott in her essay in this volume. In this context the question arises: How might an art-science public experiment such as the *Climate Garden 2085* enable relatable and concrete personal experiences?

There continues to be considerable interest, at least from science, in engaging with artists under the logic of accountability.[13] Georgia Born and Andrew Barry in their paper "Art-Science: from Public Understanding to Public Experiment" (2010) make the distinction between a project that aims to improve public understanding of – or increase public engagement with – science, and a project that is itself a public experiment. They refer to a discussion of the contrasting Greek rhetorical forms of *apodeixis* and *epideixis*. While *apodeixis* means a faithful showing of the finished knowledge or truth, *epideixis* means to make a show, to speak *to* rather than *at* an audience, i.e., to engage the audience rhetorically in a knowing process that will, as such, lead to understanding: "Where apodeixis follows the object by confirming 'what is or seems to be, epideixis *makes it be.*'" In order to further differentiate between science communication and public experiment, Born and Barry make a distinction between "the presentation of pre-existing proofs" and "managing evidence by contriving new types of obviousness."[14] Thus they argue that *apodeixis* equates to public understanding and *epideixis* equates to public experiment:

"As a form of epideixis, public experiments do not so much present existing scientific knowledge to the public, as forge relations between new knowledge, things, locations and persons that did not exist before."[15]

In this sense the *Climate Garden 2085* "manages evidence" by catalyzing new relations between time-scales, climate, place and human activity and providing relatable and concrete personal experiences.

The aim of the *Climate Garden 2085* was therefore to provide a personal experience of local food production and how it will be affected by climate change. Yet as we planned the experiment, and settled on the location of the Old Botanical

Garden with its fabulous mature trees, we realized this was also an opportunity to ask how local woodlands would be affected. To this end we expanded the curatorial scope and invited other artists to respond to a list of trees categorized into 'climate winners' and 'climate losers.' The "work" that the art did in this context was to create an embodied, i.e., physical human relationship to the trees. Integrated into a botanical tour brimming with scientific knowledge, the aesthetic responses provided 'reflexivity,' 'showing,' and knowledge from practice. Here I am referring to a definition of aesthetics from its root *aisthēsis* (*aisthētikós*, 'of sense perception'). *Aisthēsis* correlates with knowledge that can be perceived or comprehended by the senses before it is expressed in an argument or changed by writing.[16] Thus 'art aims to reflect the perceivable through perception and the experiential through experience.'[17] The resulting performances, video and audio works are described later in this volume.

The artistic strategy of the *Climate Garden 2085* greenhouses was to show the climate scenarios in an experiential form. The idea was to make this local and personal by using scenarios downscaled for northern Switzerland and growing plants that people know and eat. We also chose a mixture of plants which would be climate winners, such as soybeans and sweetcorn, and some which would be losers, such as wheat and potatoes. The particular type of greenhouse selected is commonly found in northern Swiss allotments and gardens, and together with the wooden raised beds and walkway the whole effect was designed to be familiar. It is important to emphasize that although based on scientific methods we were not aiming to recreate a scientific experiment. Indeed, the deviations from scientific studies became talking points, and we could discuss with visitors the lack of extreme weather events, short timescale, ecosystem functions, and even the fact that by 2085 the current plants will have already somewhat adapted – our model could not take this into consideration. The greenhouses contained only a minimum of textual information, as we wanted visitors to observe and feel rather than read: the environment was the narrative. In this I think we were successful. For example, visitors to the greenhouses used the terms 'clarity', 'visualization', 'demonstrative' and 'concrete' as positive attributes of the experiment. Many called it "simple but experiential" and said it made "climate change feel closer to home."

We wanted to tread the delicate line between doom and optimism, hence the use of plants whose cultivation may move northwards (e.g., sugar beet) and others which may still thrive in northern Switzerland despite increasing temperatures. Soybean is a good example of this as Switzerland currently grows 3.882 tons soy and imports 285.000 tons soy per year primarily for animal feed.[18] This provoked discussion with visitors about whether we could be self-sufficient in soy, particularly if we ate it rather than using it as animal fodder. So the story was complex: what Walzer would call a thick narrative. This proved somewhat challenging to communicate, as we noticed that many visitors expected a clear either/or statement. Here the benefit of having small groups, which allowed time for social learning, came into its own; this was also an essential part of the design strategy. We were able to find moral entry points into local dialogue by talking about local food and landscapes. Thus, although complex, a local narrative was told and it could be teased apart by making it tangible, local and relevant: this in contrast to the thick, global narrative which has proven unpersuasive. We strived to show that there were positive options despite uncertainty, but we also emphasized that, while there is uncertainty about the extent of the coming changes, the need for immediate action is indisputable.

The personal experience of immersion in an imagined future garden aimed to remedy the dissonance of climate paradox: i.e., the inability to act due to lack of personal experience. The *Climate Garden 2085* created a social learning experience by framing the story as local and providing space for discussion and reflection.

Notes

1. Hulme, 2009.
2. Fish, 2009 p. 3 in Brace and Geoghegan, 2010.
3. Brace and Geoghegan, 2010, p. 1.
4. Walzer 1994, p. 6 in Matthew, 2013, p. 93.
5. The study focuses specifically on a highly educated cohort; this is justified, as the graph in question appears in the "Summary for Policymakers" (SPM) in the *Fourth Assessment Report* (Cambridge University Press, 2007), and the sample cohort is analogous to the target audience of the SPM.
6. "Multi-model averages and assessed ranges for surface warming" SPM Fig 5, https://www.ipcc.ch/publications_and_data/ar4/wg1/en/figure-spm-5.html.
7. Schneider, 2012, in McMahon et al., 2015.
8. Stoknes, 2014, p. 6.
9. van der Linden et al., 2015, p. 759.
10. Hawkins et al., 2015, p. 331.
11. Ibid.
12. Ibid.
13. In order to understand how the *Climate Garden 2085* functions as a public experiment, we need to step back and look at art-science. Although art-science has been practiced for many years, it continually has to justify itself. A useful cartography of this has been provided by Georgia Born and Andrew Barry (2010). They show that art-science has been justified by three logical arguments. The logic of accountability points to the need for increased public understanding of science and socially robust science. The logic of innovation points to the value of art in boosting creativity in science and technology. The logic of ontology argues that if artists and scientists collaborate, they will be able to create a new understanding of the nature of art and science.
14. Cassin, 2005, p. 864, in Born and Barry, 2010, p. 265.
15. Born and Barry, 2010, p. 265.
16. Derrida quoted by Fliescher 2015 (in Mersch 2015 p. 45).
17. Mersch 2015, p. 46.
18. www.sojanetzwerk.ch (accessed 02.27.2017).

References

Born, G, and Barry, A, "Art-science: From public understanding to public experiment," in *Journal of Cultural Economy*, vol. 3 (1), 2010, pp. 103–119.

Brace, C, and Geoghegan, H, "Human geographies of climate change: Landscape, temporality, and lay knowledge," in *Progress in Human Geography*, 2010.

Fliescher, M, "Signatur Malerei Alterität," *Internationales Jahrbuch für Medienphilosophie*, vol. 1(1), 2015, pp. 67–94.

Hawkins, H, Marston, S, Ingram, M, and Straughan, E, "The Art of Socioecological Transformation," *Annals of the Association of American Geographers*, vol. 105:2, 2015, pp. 331–341.

Hulme, M, *Why We Disagree about Climate Change*, Cambridge University Press, Cambridge, 2009.

IPCC – Solomon, S (ed.), "Climate change 2007 – the physical science basis: Working group I," *Fourth Assessment Report of the IPCC*, vol. 4, Cambridge University Press, 2007.

Matthew, R, "Space Time and Scales of Human Security in Climate Change," in *Handbook on Climate Change and Human Security*, Redclift, M, and Grasso, M, (eds.), Edward Elgar Publishing, 2013.

Mersch, D, *Epistemologies of Aesthetics*, Diaphanes, University of Chicago Press, 2015.

McMahon, R, Stauffacher, M, and Knutti, R, "The unseen uncertainties in climate change: reviewing comprehension of an IPCC scenario graph," in *Climatic Change*, vol.133, 2015, pp. 141–154.

Stoknes, PE, "Rethinking climate communications and the 'psychological climate paradox,' " in *Energy Research & Social Science*, vol. 1, 2014, pp. 161–170.

van der Linden, S, Maibach, E, and Leiserowitz, A, "Improving Public Engagement With Climate Change: Five 'Best Practice' Insights From Psychological Science," in *Perspectives on Psychological Science*, vol. 10(6), 2015, pp. 758–763.

Connected to place: Climate change on global and local scales

Katie Horgan

Katie Horgan is a doctoral researcher studying how a suite of research sites is providing ecosystem service benefits to populations on different scales and levels. Her background is in forestry and community engagement in the UK, largely working with urban communities in the management of their woodlands. She trained in countryside management and worked for local authorities and government agencies as a ranger in a number of different settings. She is interested in how it is possible to engage with individuals and communities to create active, connected biodiversity conservation measures that are mutually beneficial, self-sustaining and long-term.

Our relationships with our planet are intricate and multi-layered, and have been formed over millennia.[1] Across ecosystems, societies and cultures, we express a sense of connection with our 'place.' How we speak about the natural world, the ways in which we interact with soil and water, plants and wildlife, all reflect these deep connections to, and care for, place. Climate and land-use are shifting, and changes to weather patterns, seasons, agriculture and habitats all alter how we interact with planet Earth. Whether gardening or gathering in a changing climate, connection and care are as important as technology if we are to continue to adapt to our changing planet.[2]

Through interviews with people working and researching in different parts of the world,[3] I have been able to trace some of these connections and perceptions of change, alongside indications of a continual ability to adapt. In this essay I would like to share stories from the Arctic Circle, the Tibetan plateau, Switzerland, the Seychelles, and Malaysia: stories of peoples' relation to place, and how a changing climate is already affecting the plants and animals with which they are connected.

People living beyond the Arctic Circle, around the Kytalyk Resource Reserve in Sakha Republic (Siberia), have found ways to live in an environment that is dark and frozen for at least half of the year.[4] While they now receive goods from around the world, their connections with the land and its resources remain. They collect mushrooms and berries for subsistence and because they are culturally important – making jam to give to relatives and visitors is part of their social relations. Reindeer herding is also still integral to their lives, and despite dramatic changes in how this is practiced, people and communities working with reindeer continue to "use everything from reindeer." Communities are also very dependent on fish as a food source, with fishing a regular and important activity. People commute to fishing villages in the summer and stay there until the winter. As one person said, "Fish is life," showing the role of the rivers on which they depend for food, driftwood, transport and winter roads – "everything comes from the river … Local people couldn't do without it." A deeper sense of place is reflected in the symbolic importance of the Siberian crane or *kytalyk*. The Resource Reserve was established by local people to protect this species, and one person described the area as a "reservoir of traditional practices," centered on the Siberian crane.[5] Another mentioned the traditional dances based on the crane's mating dance, describing this as "a powerful symbol" derived from "a spiritual bird."

Similar kinds of connection are also apparent on the alpine grasslands of the Tibetan plateau in China.[6] Here people continue to collect wild mushrooms and plants for food and medicinal use. This includes the caterpillar fungus (*Cordyceps sinensis*[7]), silverweed (*Potentilla anserina*), and gentian (*Gentiana* spp.). Residents of the plateau depend directly on this grassland habitat; as one interviewee said, "It sustains the living." People herd yaks (*Bos grunniens*) and Tibetan sheep, and harvest crops such as highland barley (*Hordeum vulgare var. coeleste*) and oats (*Avena sativa*). The use of natural resources extends to "soil … used to make bricks," and "dried cow dung and sheep dung for burning and warming." The connections are reflected in the cultural importance of yaks and the caterpillar fungus, both are "the symbol of Qinghai."

It is not only across these vast, wild landscapes that elements of traditional practices are maintained. In and around the temperate forests of Switzerland people continue to collect wild plants for food, such as wild garlic (*Allium ursinum*), berries and mushrooms. In Canton Aargau, mushroom collection is regulated by the *Pilzkontrolle* office, suggesting the continuing importance of this activity. While it, too, is strictly regulated, hunting of wild animals including deer (*Capreolus capreolus*) and boar (*Sus scrofa*) is an important activity, both for food and for pest control. This is connected with the agriculture around the forest, where farmers harvest a variety of crops. As one person said, "It is important for small villages." The forest, growing on a distinctive limestone ridge, the last outcrop of the Jura mountain chain, is also a well-known hiking area, making it "important for recreation and the local economy" but also "for the landscape and for the people."[8]

The importance of landscape and biodiversity to people's lives is echoed far out in the Indian Ocean. The raised coral atoll of Aldabra 400 km from the main Seychelles Islands has many endemic species. Before 1982, when the atoll became a World Heritage Site, the Aldabra giant tortoise (*Aldabrachelys gigantea*), green turtle (*Chelonia mydas*), flightless Aldabra rails (*Dryolimnas aldabranus*), and ibis (*Threskiornis aethiopicus abbotti*), as well as bird's eggs, were harvested. Now, imbued with their own "stories and folklore," the Aldabra giant tortoise and Aldabra rail have become national emblems displayed on coins and stamps. For the small group of people who now live in the research community on the atoll, the abundant fish are essential "for subsistence." However, fishing is more important than simply providing protein. One interviewee described how necessary it is to "reduce boredom, therefore it's recreationally important." And the name of the atoll probably connects to a time when islands were important navigational aids to early Arabian explorers. One interviewee suggested "Aldabra" was derived from *alhadra*, the Arabic for green, because "there's a green reflection on the clouds from the lagoon."

Tropical forests also sustain many peoples and cultures.[9] In and around the forests of Malaysia, local people continue to collect plants and fruits to eat, including *petai* bitter bean (*Parkia speciosa*), *keledang* (*Artocarpus lanceifolius*), *ulam* salad (*Centella asiatica*) and *kerdas* (*Archidendron bubalinum*). They also collect fungi, using the traditional local knowledge that is essential for people to know "which are the poisonous ones." Shifting agricultural production continues around the edges of the forests, with smallholders cultivating rice, fruit, vegetables and oil palm, and hunting around the forest edges. Pigs may be food and monkeys may be pests, but the connections to the forest and its inhabitants run deeper than this. The white-handed gibbon, "rhino, elephant[10] – these are symbolic" in Malaysia. While communities and farming practices may have altered how people use the forests – especially as they are often reserves – indigenous people still "use forest for everything" and have a "close relationship" with it. Some interviewees made careful references to "Tebu places" – places where respect must be shown to the forest. For some, there are other reasons why forests are important: "People escape here to feel better … Without the forest we would be living with no meaning."

These close relationships with land, with wildlife, and within ecosystems mean that people notice changes. In Kytalyk, people have noticed changes to reindeer migration patterns; they say "they do not see so many wild reindeer coming through." This is echoed in comments from the Tibetan Plateau, where people suggest that "unique natural scenes seem to be fewer and fewer." In a temperate Swiss forest, long-term residents have seen seasonal patterns shift, raising "questions about how the forest is managed." On Aldabra, the food people eat has changed, as tortoises and turtles are protected, and interviewees notice the direct impacts of climate change: "Beach erosion is a natural process – but some sand does not come back. We lost the old cemetery." Changes to wildlife in Malaysian forests also don't go unnoticed. Logging has in the past led to the loss of big trees, while the "bird population seems to have declined" and only small mammals are present.[11] It isn't just the wildlife that has changed, with one interviewee describing increased flooding in his village. Human movement is impacted by environmental and socio-economic change: for example, indigenous territories become state owned, government land becomes privately owned, and small-scale subsistence farming is swallowed up by large oil palm plantations.[12] As a result, people move, looking for new opportunities in different sectors. This change is illustrated by comments from Malaysian Borneo about the indigenous Orang Sunai, who no longer subsist inside the forest "but live around the edges and around Sabah." They now have more settled, agricultural, and mixed livelihoods.

Some of these changes may be part of quite natural processes, as societies and communities shift to more stable lifestyles that are less dependent on their surrounding environments. However, some changes are worrying, bringing threats to health, to livelihoods, and to ecosystems themselves.[13] Changes to the tundra system around Kytalyk affect indigenous people and traditional ways of life, where many people remain dependent in some way on the system. These changes range from altered reindeer migration patterns, through earlier and less predictable snow melt destroying winter roads, to changes to fish stocks in rivers. The changes are system-wide; as one interviewee said, global warming is "unstoppable there," for as the soil warms it releases CO_2 and although this is invisible, "it has a huge impact for the world."[14] There are concerns also about social changes, with younger generations disconnecting from their traditions – "children did not even know what the reindeer look like" – and migrating to the towns for better employment opportunities.[15]

The grasslands of the Tibetan plateau are also "sensitive to global change and threatened by anthropogenic activities." Interviewees expressed concern about the potential CO_2 release from this area with climate warming. Others perceive that, once it is damaged, it is very difficult to restore such a unique landscape. The biggest harm noticed in our Swiss forests is the increasing prevalence of ticks carrying both Lyme disease and encephalitis.[16]

On Aldabra the threats are varied, with the boundary between land and sea constantly shifting. "Coastal erosion means it is always moving back and forth. Climate change and sea level rise make this worse." The plants and animals introduced for production, to feed the early workers, and by accident, have been a significant threat to such a sensitive ecosystem. These include rats, goats, cats, invasive birds, nineteen plant species and one species of gecko.[17]

While not as exposed as a coral atoll, tropical forests are also perceived as subject to definite threats. Interviewees often note the lack of animals due to deforestation, and the negative changes in air temperature and humidity outside the forest. Increased erosion and muddy rivers are seen to be a consequence of the spread of oil palm plantations. People were often very clear that the forest is necessary to maintain a clean, functioning system: "Without forest there would be a lot of mud in the river. When trees fall down the river is more muddy." They recognize that the forest is "a natural ecosystem, but if this gets disturbed these services are also disturbed."[18]

This seems to paint a very negative picture of a changing world; but people, communities and ecosystems are adaptable. Our dependencies change, building on past knowledge while adopting new technologies, practices and traditions. For example, while people in Siberia still collect berries and mushrooms, these are now "important, but probably not for sustenance." However, collecting berries remains a seasonal tradition. People also combine the old and the new, building fishing huts from "peat and turf over chicken wire" and continue to use reindeer skins where they can. Traditional knowledge is preserved, with reindeer herders organizing annual events to teach people in the villages their traditions. In China, old and new uses are found for natural resources. Pikas (*Ochotona dauurica*), marmots (*Marmota bobak*) and false zokhor (*Myospalax aspalax*) are collected for pest control and food, but also for scientific research. In fact, the current importance of the area for research is in part what is helping to preserve it. Some adaptations are in response to very recent changes, such as the noise pollution from airports and motorways. Laegern Forest in Switzerland can be "extremely important … when you are in it. You can not see or hear the road." This adaptability extends to dealing with other human-caused problems. On Aldabra, many of the invasive species have now been eradicated and people are "very careful about which seeds are brought in." While fish are important for the small community there, they have learned to harvest carefully without disturbing the system or creating by-catch. As one person said, people recognize that "in the past human beings were reckless, careless,"[19] but now Aldabra is "a success story."[19] Sometimes it isn't possible to avoid land use change; often we need agricultural land rather than forest. People interviewed in Malaysia find value in both, seeing that having oil palm and forest next to each other can be beneficial: "You see more wild animals in oil palm near forest than you see in the forest because they come out for food – it's hard for them between seeding times. It's a good symbiosis … it's good for my crops." The adaptability of other species is noticed in other ways, for example the monitor lizard (*Varanus salvator*) that "tidies up scraps after tourists – you always see them at Latak Waterfall." Finally, global change – whether this is change to the climate or change in how land is used – has also brought a greater awareness of the bigger picture, enhancing the importance of one's own place: "Every place is a piece of the bigger jigsaw puzzle, it all does something. It's really important to contribute to your piece of the puzzle. You know you can have sand from the Sahara desert on the roof of the car and you realize it's not so far away" (noticed by a forester in the Laegern forest).

Above all, these stories have shown how our relationships with wildlife, with gathering, with keeping our hands in the soil, are constantly being renewed. Many people see themselves as guardians of wildlife and the ecosystem, valuing what has now become rare. As wildlife becomes scarcer, it becomes more mystical, preserved in traditions such as the Crane dance, giving a reason for the creation of reserves to protect it, and still providing spaces for traditional knowledge to be experienced. We will always be dependent on the Earth for our own sustenance, and we must be able to develop a deep relationship with her. Preserving spaces also protects our connections and traditions, and helps us to understand that in a changing world our gardens can grow if we listen to and care for them: "It's special but it isn't unique. The forest grew into my heart."

This project was supported by the University of Zurich Research Priority Programme, Global Change and Biodiversity
www.gcb.uzh.ch

Notes

1   Ruddimann et al., 2015.
2   Steffen et al., 2015.
3   Russia (Sakha Republic): Kytalyk Resource Reserve; China (Qinghai Province, Tibetan plateau): Haibei Alpine Meadow Ecosystem Research Station; Switzerland: Laegern Forest; Seychelles: Aldabra Atoll; Malaysia: Pasoh Forest Reserve (Peninsular), Danum Valley Conservation Area (Sabah), Lambir Hills National Park (Sarawak).
4   Beltrán and Phillips, 2000.
5   *Leucogeranus leucogeranus*.
6   Zhao and Zhou, 1999.
7   Now *Ophiocordyceps sinensis*, caterpillar fungus, used for 2000 years in Chinese medicine.
8   Balvanera et al., 2006.
9   Buschbacher, 1990, Edwards et al., 2014.
10 *Dicerorhinus sumatrensis harissoni*; *elephas maximus borneensis*.
11 Harrison et al., 2013.
12 Ichikawa, 2006.
13 Lal, 2009.
14 Post et al., 2009, Kintisch, 2015.
15 Xanthaki, 2004.
16 Rieille, 2014.
17 Harper and Bunbury, 2015.
18 Struebig et al., 2015.
19 Stoddart, 1971.
20 Gaymer, 1966.

References

Balvanera, P, Pfisterer, AB, Buchmann, N, He, JS, Nakashizuka, T, Raffaelli, D, and Schmid, B, "Quantifying the evidence for biodiversity effects on ecosystem functioning and services: Biodiversity and ecosystem functioning/services," in *Ecology Letters*, vol. 9 (10), 2006, pp. 1146–1156.

Beltrán, J, and Phillips, A (eds.), *Indigenous and Traditional Peoples and Protected Areas*, Cambridge: IUCN Publications Services, 2000.

Buschbacher, RJ, "Natural Forest Management in the Humid Tropics: Ecological, Social, and Economic Considerations," in *AMBIO*, vol. 19 (5), 1990, pp. 253–258.

Edwards, DP, Gilroy, JJ, Woodcock, P, Edwards, FA, Larsen, TH, Andrews, DJR, Derhé, MA, Docherty, TDS, Hsu, WW, Mitchell, SL, Ota, T, Williams, LJ, Laurance, WF, Hamer, KC, and Wilcove, DS, "Land-sharing versus land-sparing logging: reconciling timber extraction with biodiversity conservation," in *Global Change Biology*, vol. 20 (1), 2014, pp. 183–191.

Gaymer, R, "Aldabra – The Case for Conserving this Coral Atoll," in *Fauna and Flora International*, vol. 8 (6), 1966, pp. 348–352.

Harper, GA, and Bunbury, N, "Invasive rats on tropical islands: Their population biology and impacts on native species," in *Global Ecology and Conservation*, vol. 3, 2015, pp. 607–627.

Harrison, RD, Tan, S, Plotkin, JB, Slik, F, Detto, M, Brenes, T, Itoh, A, and Davies, SJ, "Consequences of defaunation for a tropical tree community," in *Ecology Letters*, vol. 16 (5), 2013, pp. 687–694.

Ichikawa, M, "Large-scale forest development and land use by the Iban around the Lambir Hills National Park," in *Proceedings of International Symposium on Forest Ecology, Hydrometeorology and Forest Ecosystem Rehabilitation in Sarawak*, 2006.

Kintisch, E, "Boom & bust in the Great White North," in *Science*, vol. 349 (6248), 2015, pp. 578–581.

Lal, R, "Tragedy of the Global Commons: Soil, Water and Air," in *Climate Change, Intercropping, Pest Control and Beneficial Microorganisms*, edited by Eric Lichtfouse, Dordrecht: Springer, 2009, 9–11.

Post, E, Forchhammer, MC, Bret-Harte, MS, Callaghan, TV, Christensen, TR, Elberling, B, Fox, AD, Gilg, O, Hik, DS, Hoye, TT, Ims, RA, Jeppesen, E, Klein, DR, Madsen, J, McGuire, AD, Rysgaard, S, Schindler, DE, Stirling, I, Tamstorf, MP, Tyler, NJC, van der Wal, R, Welker, J, Wookey, PA, Schmidt, NM, and Aastrup, P, "Ecological Dynamics Across the Arctic Associated with Recent Climate Change," in *Science*, vol. 325 (5946), 2009, pp. 1355–1358.

Rieille, N, Bressanelli, S, Freire, CCM, Arcioni, S, Gern, L, Péter, O, and Voordouw, MJ, "Prevalence and phylogenetic analysis of tick-borne encephalitis virus (TBEV) in field-collected ticks (*Ixodes ricinus*) in southern Switzerland," in *Parasites & Vectors*, vol. 7 (443), 2014.

Ruddiman, WF, Ellis, EC, Kaplan, JO, and Fuller, DQ, "Defining the epoch we live in," in *Science*, vol. 348 (6230), 2015, pp. 38–39.

Steffen, W, Richardson, K, Rockstrom, J, Cornell, SE, Fetzer, I, Bennett, EM, Biggs, R, Carpenter, SR, de Vries, W, de Wit, CA, Folke, C, Gerten, D, Heinke, J, Mace, GM, Persson, LM, Ramanathan, V, Reyers, B, and Sorlin, S, "Planetary boundaries: Guiding human development on a changing planet," in *Science*, vol. 347 (6223), 2015, pp. 736–746.

Stoddart, DR, "Settlement, Development and Conservation of Aldabra. A Discussion on the Results of the Royal Society Expedition to Aldabra 1967–68," in *Philosophical Transactions of the Royal Society of London. Series B, Biological Sciences*, vol. 260 (836), 1971, pp. 611–628.

Struebig, MJ, Wilting, A, Gaveau, DLA, Meijaard, E, Smith, RJ, Fischer, M, Metcalfe, K, and Kramer-Schadt, S, "Targeted Conservation to Safeguard a Biodiversity Hotspot from Climate and Land-Cover Change," in *Current Biology*, vol. 25 (3), 2015, pp. 372–378.

Xanthaki, A, "Indigenous Rights in the Russian Federation: The Rights Case of Numerically Small Peoples of the Russian North, Siberia, and Far East," in *Human Rights Quarterly*, vol. 26 (1), 2004, pp. 74–105.

Zhao, XQ, and Zhou, XM, "Ecological Basis of Alpine Meadow Ecosystem Management in Tibet: Haibei Alpine Meadow Ecosystem Research Station," in *AMBIO*, vol. 28 (8), 1999, pp. 642–647.

Botanical time travel to unspectacular climatic futures

Emily Eliza Scott

Emily Eliza Scott is an interdisciplinary scholar, artist, and former park ranger who focuses on contemporary art and design practices that engage pressing (political) ecological issues, often with the intent to actively transform real-world conditions. Currently a postdoctoral fellow in the architecture department at ETH Zurich, she teaches on subjects ranging from the concept of "post-nature," to institutional critique, to emergent geographies of climate change.

Upon stepping into one of two identical structures that comprise the *Climate Garden 2085* – themselves situated within the highly pertinent context of the Old Botanical Gardens at the University of Zurich and on the scale of domestic greenhouses in a backyard or one of the "Schrebergärten" (community owned allotments) of German-speaking Europe[1] – I immediately sensed a subtle change in the ambient air temperature and humidity. On a warm summer day, the contrast was not by any means a shock to the system, but enough to constitute a perceptible shift from the environment outside the walls of the makeshift building to its interior. Before me, two linear plant beds extended along either side along the architecture's length, each brimming with a mixture of vaguely familiar-looking plants. While it was clear that a botanical experiment was under way in this natural-light-infused laboratory, identifying any visible difference between the parallel parcels (one a control and the other a variable?) proved trickier. Indeed, the "results" of this display, at least to my untrained eyes, remained largely ambiguous, or even illegible.

From prior information as well as that provided on site (e.g., in a free brochure), I knew that this public art installation set out to demonstrate what a typical Swiss garden, containing plants such as chard, sunflowers, and wheat, might look like under two possible Intergovernmental Panel of Climate Change (IPCC) scenarios for the year 2085, as defined by the downscaling for northeast Switzerland by Meteoschweiz/ETH CH-2011. The less drastic case – and the one most discussed and publicized as a policy target at the 2015 United Nations Climate Change Conference (COP21) in Paris – would entail a 2°C global-average temperature increase; meanwhile, in the more dire case, a 4°C warming would ensue. Two horticultural plots were accordingly planted and maintained under controlled climatic conditions within the *Climate Garden 2085*, which also took into account the predicted decline in rainfall for the Zurich region some sixty-eight years from now, the farthest reach of these scenarios' respective calendars. (Plants in one row of each hut received 30% less water than in the other.)

What interests me, first and foremost, is the way this project translates the climate scenarios into built design, thereby opening the possibility for sensorial experiences of various hypothetical, not-so-distant futures.[2] While directly engaging with climate science, the *Climate Garden 2085* installation is not factual, per se, but rather involves the embodiment of calculated projections into tangible, empirical form. It exists somewhere between the model and the material world, in other words, raising fertile questions about the convoluted relationship between the two. Equally significant, it exists between the future and the present, implicitly framing nature as a historical rather than a timelessly stable entity, and, moreover, one that is thoroughly enmeshed with human action.

Climate science – and Earth systems science, more generally – is itself an elaborate construct, or a "vast machine," in the words of Paul Edwards, whose monumental study provides a "historical account of climate science as a global knowledge infrastructure," and asks, among other fundamental questions: "How did 'the world' become a system?"[3] As a historian of science, Edwards is concerned with how we have come to know such a composite and unwieldy thing as the atmosphere and, by extension, its modification by anthropogenic influences. He notes the central role of the model in this trajectory, especially since the 1960s, when (at the same time as the interrelated rise of cybernetics and a vivid ecological imagination) it "outpaced empirically based knowledge of the global climate."[4] One reason for the prevalence of modeling in climate science, perhaps too obvious to state, is the mind-boggling number of factors in play; another, the temporal and spatial scales involved. Much that we know, as a result, takes place in algorithms and on screens – which is not to say that the direct observation of climate change is impossible (think of the countless reports in recent decades of strange weather events or the appearance of migratory species and spring blooms weeks before their expected arrival dates), but that empirical evidence, by virtue of its inevitable restrictedness in place and time, and likewise its isolation to that which is graspable via the senses, only gets us so far. Speaking like a true Earth systems scientist, Gavin Schmidt, director of NASA's Goddard Institute for Space Studies and Columbia University's Earth Institute and co-founder of the blog RealClimate, stresses the inherent limits of direct observation for understanding a phenomenon as complex and all-encompassing as climate change: "You can't understand [it] in pieces. It's the whole, or it's nothing."[5] Climate change deniers, of course, have capitalized wildly on the difficulty, or even impossibility, of "proving" this process-force by way of simple and straightforward evidence (despite the fact that such types of evidence are ultimately incompatible with the subject at hand).

Climate Garden 2085 acknowledges the coexistent values of expert and citizen-based, or "ground-up," climate intelligence, thereby suggesting that some of the legitimacy granted widely to the former be extended to the latter. Certainly, it seeks to facilitate discussion and debate in the public realm around the many questions catalyzed by global warming, including the role of the perceptual as well as individual and collective environmental memory in addressing them. This is underscored by the project's emphasis on hands-on pedagogy. Over the course of its half-year tenure in Zurich, the site hosted regular public programs, ranging from interactive theater for children to shared meals and informal talks by scientists. Schläpfer-Miller prefers the term "public experiment" to characterize her endeavor, which emphasizes its embrace of ambiguity and slippage as opposed to clarity, or easy digestibility. Such a descriptor additionally distinguishes this work from "science communication," which remains wedded, or even subservient, to the domain of science and its fiercely defended "matters of fact."[6]

As art, *Climate Garden 2085* is more invested in cultivating questions than answers. Its attention to experimentation, exchange, and observation highlights the extent to which techno-scientific versus public and embodied approaches to climate change open onto different horizons of questions. The architect and theorist Meredith Miller, among others, has written about the potential of speculative cultural practices to provide a much needed "alternative to the abstracting tendencies of [the] data-focused [ones]" that dominate mainstream representations of climate change.[7] Among the endless, and often existential, questions sparked by the "wicked problem" (or, more accurately, bundle of wicked problems) that is climate change are: What does it mean to know the climate and who claims the right to pursue and articulate such knowledge?[8] Where are the edges of the human? How does human history fit into both deep time and nonhuman time? Is a term like "nature" still meaningful in the face of growing evidence that humans are affecting the planet on the scale of its Earth systems, a notion captured by the concept of the "Anthropocene"? If we want to adopt *that* term, how, exactly, does it relate to climate change? What forms of analysis and representation are adequate to this moment of "great derangement," as the Indian author Amitav Ghosh has recently painted it, including the radical asymmetries between those responsible for climate change and those who bear its brunt?[9]

In a number of fields spanning the arts, humanities, and social sciences, the term "nature" has come under increasing pressure, and in notably quicker step with the emergence and rapid spread of the Anthropocene concept. Many now argue that "nature" carries too much ideological baggage not to be suspect – whether because it is fatally tied to the idea of something "out there" and other to the human, associated with the myth of a stable background or reference point, or because it fails to reflect the circumstances of its own making (i.e., its *unnaturalness*). Even within the discipline of ecology, some forward-thinking scientists are pushing for an abandonment of the idea of a baseline nature against which deviation is evaluated, pointing instead to the "ecological novelty," or perpetual dynamism and intricate human-nonhuman interface, which constitutes all environments today.[10]

In art and, especially, architecture, nature has nonetheless often persisted as a normative or essentialist category. At the other extreme, an almost ecstatic embrace of the "post-natural" (or "new nature," "second nature," etc.) is palpable and pervasive. In some cases, this verges on a crude fetishism of the artificial, biotechnological, monstrous, etc., reminiscent of the science-fiction genre and amounting to a profoundly uncritical flight from politics. Within architecture, the rhetoric of post-naturalism has, at times, also seemed to provide a convenient excuse from the rigors and responsibilities of context-sensitivity, or to support a *tabula rasa* approach that makes modernist master plans look downright nuanced. (The age-old celebration of autonomy, thinly disguised as the new.) More optimistically, the architectural historian and theorist David Gissen locates in some strains of contemporary architectural practice a kind of critical post-naturalism, the astuteness and reflexivity of which lie precisely in its orientation toward history. Such a mode begins with the recognition that nature is always contingent – an idea that is humanly constructed and therefore necessarily culturally and historically specific as well as changeable. He writes: "[…] every epoch, era, and urban or architectural episteme arrived at particular views, uses, or conceptions of 'nature' […]. […] History can be visualized within things that make nature appear as the problem it is, versus our given reality."[11]

Before circling back to *Climate Garden 2085*, I wish to briefly consider two artworks that "make nature appear as the problem it is" by dealing with it in historical terms. More specifically, both incorporate what I am calling botanical time travel and thus serve as proximate and elucidating reference points for the *Climate Garden 2085* project. *Time Landscape* (1965/1978 – present), by the New York-based artist Alan Sonfist, has become a fixture in canonical accounts of environmental, or "eco-," art. First conceived in 1965 and executed in 1978, this rectangular plot – roughly fourteen by sixty-one meters and containing over two hundred plant species that were native to Manhattan in pre-Colonial times – still occupies, albeit in somewhat ramshackle shape, the bustling, northeast corner of La Guardia Place and West Houston Street in SoHo. To a large extent, it now resembles any number of other urban "pocket parks" in and around the city, its botanical uniqueness easily overlooked, not least owing to the scant knowledge of local natural history on the part of most passers-by (itself a partial function of urbanization's tendency to displace any and all that is not explicitly human). The central trope here is anachronism, or the introduction of something out of time into the present. Sonfist himself, in a 1968 essay, explained his intent to "roll back the clock and show the layers of time before the concrete of the city."[12] The temporal dissonance of his gesture was only amplified by the plot's designation as a historical landmark in 1988 by the New York City Landmarks Preservation Commission. As others have noted, *Time Landscape* has a strong commemorative component.[13] Again, in Sonfist's words: "As in war monuments that record the life and death of soldiers, the life and death of natural phenomena such as rivers, springs, and natural outcroppings need to be remembered. Public art can be a reminder that the city was once a forest or a marsh."[14] While his artwork involves the reconstruction of an erased past, *Climate Garden 2085*, somewhat differently – as we know – is pitched toward projected futures, namely, those calculated by scientists in their attempt to understand how climate change will unfold in coming decades.

We might also ponder the American artist Mark Dion's *Neukom Vivarium* (2006), which is perhaps less about time travel than space travel, or the re-contextualization of a living ecosystem from the forest to the city, and from an outdoor to an indoor environment. The centerpiece, or protagonist, of *Neukom Vivarium* is a fallen Western hemlock tree that was transported to the apparatus-intensive confines of a greenhouse – more accurately, a "vivarium," or facility meant for researching live flora and fauna – at the Olympic Sculpture Park in Seattle, Washington. While, at first glance, this project may seem hopeful in its spotlight on the way that decay supports new life – indeed, within the unfathomably intricate ecosystem of a coastal temperate rainforest, so-called "nurse logs," or dead and downed trees, are a primary driver of regeneration – it is also unmistakably macabre. The artist himself has referred to the vivarium as "a sort of Sleeping Beauty coffin," and proposed, "You should look at this and get the impression of someone in the hospital under an oxygen tent."[15] The profusion of technological equipment filling this laboratory-like container no doubt evokes a life-support system that holds this rich multispecies complex in a state of perpetual presence. As such, it reminds us of the incredible effort, if not ultimate futility, of attempting to replicate the dizzyingly elaborate systems of the natural world – this, moreover, in the context of the already acute biodiversity loss caused by climate change, among other human forces, which many are now convinced represents the sixth mass extinction in the Earth's history.[16] No wonder Dion has likened his gesture to a *memento mori*.

As suggested above, *Climate Garden 2085* inhabits a time span somewhere between the foreseeable future, or one close enough that we can almost imagine it, and the current moment. More to the point, it aims to wrest various likely futures concretely and viscerally into the present. Such an act, among other things, intimates that our actions in the present will have a direct bearing on the future, both immediate and distant, thus opening the present as a space for action. In her own essay within this book, Schläpfer-Miller addresses the deeply consequential contradiction between the relatively ample public knowledge about climate change and the negligible public action in response to it as yet. She looks, in part, to psychologists' explanations for the barriers to successful climate change communication, one being the commonplace (mis-) perception that it remains remote as an issue, and, another, that "scenarios *may or may not come to pass.*" The *Climate Garden 2085* project, in this sense, possesses a distinctly ameliorative intent: to bring the subject of climate change, along with its attendant urgencies, to the fore and, moreover, to highlight the need for engaging with it seriously in the here and now.

The garden may seem an unexpected medium through which to grapple with potent crises of the present day. The art historian TJ Demos, however, has identified it as one of crucial contemporary importance:

"Gardens may seem irrelevant to our world of crises and emergencies [...] but in fact they concern the most urgent of global conflicts – including the corporate financialization of nature, realized by the patenting of genetically modified seeds by agriculture and pharmaceutical corporations; the production of greenhouse gas emissions, via a monoculture- and export-based agribusiness reliant on the fossil-fuelled transportation industry and chemical fertilizers; and the destruction of unions and small-scale farmers, displaced by the mechanization and monopoly ownership of the means of production."[17]

In a largely critical review of the 2012 iteration of dOCUMENTA (13), in Kassel, Germany, he noted the remarkable abundance of garden-based projects and their seeming summoning of timely matters, even if many, to his mind, failed to convey discernible positions with regard to them. (His sharpest criticism was saved for the curatorial team's wishy-washy-ness.)

The garden, following Demos, represents (or holds special potential to represent) expressly not an escape from the contemporary, but rather a crux of the present and its myriad, thorny challenges. Among them is the paradoxical reality that despite ever more sophisticated means to understand and track the environment, including the modeling of future scenarios, the human-natural world is undergoing immensely accelerated and unpredictable transformations at the hands of these very "advancements." And, such derangements pose tremendous hurdles to our ability to read the world around us. It is highly fitting, then, that the difference between a 2°C and 4°C warming – as embodied in the *Climate Garden's* meticulously planted and tended botanical plots – appears unclear. Indeed, the most radical aspect of this project may be its evocation of unspectacular climatic futures. In contradistinction to the kinds of eye-grabbing images of melting ice caps, expanding deserts, and inundated metropolises that have come to dominate the visual culture of climate change, *Climate Garden 2085* hints that this process-force will unfold in far less dramatic and scenic ways: for example, with the gradual disappearance of one plant species and its replacement by another in everyday urban habitats such as Zurich.

Alan Sonfist, *Time Landscape* (1965–present), indigenous materials, 45′ × 200′ (14 × 61 meters), New York City. Courtesy of the artist.

Mark Dion, *Neukom Vivarium* (2006), mixed media installation, greenhouse structure: 80 ft. L overall. Photo: Paul Macapia. Installation view: Seattle Art Museum, Seattle Washington, 2006. Seattle Art Museum, Gift of Sally and William Neukom, American Express Company, Seattle Garden Club, Mark Torrance Foundation and Committee of 33, in honor of the 75th Anniversary of the Seattle Art Museum. Courtesy the artist and Tanya Bonakdar Gallery, New York

Notes

1. For a brief introduction to the Schreber Garden, see Turowski, "The Schreber Garden," *Cabinet*, vol. 6, 2002.
2. The curator and philosopher Dehlia Hannah has assembled a small collection of "model climates" by artists and architects on her website, which serves as a fascinating set of sibling projects to *Climate Garden 2085*.
3. Edwards, 2010, p. 8, p. 3; see also the very useful review of Edwards' book by McKenzie Wark, "Climate Science as Sensory Infrastructure," in *The White Review* no. 11, 2014.
4. Edwards insists that the information derived from models and that from the so-called real world are not dichotomous, but rather, closely entangled: Edwards, xiii-xiv.
5. Schmidt, "The Emergent Patterns of Climate Change," TED Talks, published May 1, 2014.
6. Here I refer to the distinction between "matters of fact" and "matters of concern" made by Latour in his essay, "Why Has Critique Run Out of Steam?," in *Critical Inquiry*, 2004, pp. 225–248.
7. Miller, 2016, p. 71; see also my own essay in the same volume, "Archives of the Present-Future: Climate Change and Representational Breakdown," pp. 130–140.
8. Ways of knowing are always contingent upon specific historical, cultural, and ideological contexts. The 2010 documentary film *Inuit Knowledge and Climate Change* (Isama Productions) draws this point into vivid view.
9. See the chapter by Caroline Wiedmer within this volume for a more detailed discussion of Ghosh's book.
10. For example: Kueffer, "Ecological Novelty: Towards an Interdisciplinary Understanding of Ecological Change in the Anthropocene," in *Grounding Global Climate Change: Contributions from the Social and Cultural Sciences*, eds. Greschke and Tischler, New York: Springer, 2014, pp. 19–37.
11. Gissen, 2015, p. 6; of parallel interest is Lutticken's "Unnatural History," in *New Left Review*, vol. 45, 2007, pp. 115–131.
12. Sonfist, 1968, p. 546.
13. For instance, Slifkin, "Alan Sonfist: Natural History," in *Alan Sonfist: Natural History*, eds. Slifkin, Snyder, and Tepper, Portland, Oregon: Companion Editions, 2015, pp. 19–45.
14. Sonfist, 1968, p. 542.
15. ART21 interview with Mark Dion on *Neukom Vivarium* (undated).
16. See Kolbert, *The Sixth Extinction: An Unnatural History*, New York: Picador, 2015. The art historian Miwon Kwon has written about the ways that Dion takes up contemporary ecological issues as being human-natural in character. Miwon Kwon, "Unnatural Tendencies: Scientific Guises of Mark Dion," *Forum International*, 1993, p. 41.
17. TJ Demos, 2012.

References

Edwards, P, *A Vast Machine: Computer Models, Climate Data, and the Politics of Global Warming*, Cambridge, MA: MIT Press, 2010.

Demos, TJ, "Gardens Beyond Eden: Bio-aesthetics, Eco-Futurism, and Dystopia at dOCUMENTA (13)," in *The Brooklyn Rail*, vol. 4, 2012.

Gissen, D, "Nature's Historical Crisis," in *Journal of Architectural Education,* vol. 69, (1), 2015.

Miller, M, "Views From the Plastisphere: A Preface to Post-Rock Architecture," in *Climates: Architecture & the Planetary Imaginary*, ed. James Graham, New York and Zurich: Columbia Books on Architecture and the City with Lars Müller Publishers, 2016.

Sonfist, A, "Natural Phenomena as Public Monuments" (1968), in *Theories and Documents of Contemporary Art: a Sourcebook of Artists' Writings*, eds. Kristine Stiles and Peter Selz, Berkeley: Univ. of California Press, 1996.

An ethical discourse on CO$_2$ reduction

Melanie Paschke

Melanie Paschke, who has a PhD in ecology and environmental sciences, is Director of Education at the Zurich-Basel Plant Science Center. She has led the development of higher education programs there for more than ten years, including the PhD programs in Plant Sciences and Science and Policy. She has a track record as educator in several areas of academic professional conduct and transferable skill development, with more than 30 training workshops, summer schools and seminars taught in previous years. Her focus is on ethics and research integrity in plant sciences.

The Paris Climate Agreement of 2015 again set 2°C as the upper limit of median global warming to which all subscribing nations aspired. But even this limit requires immediate action from us on many different levels. On the one hand, global CO$_2$ emissions must be reduced to 350 ppm; on the other, society must be prepared for the necessary adaptation to these conditions.

Climate Garden 2085 made the impact of climate change visual and palpable. Follow-up conversations with visitors regularly produced questions about possible strategies for CO$_2$ reduction and about the distribution of the burden brought about by climate change. In both respects, acceptance of necessary measures can be facilitated by social discourse.

There are three distinct – but not necessarily mutually exclusive – approaches to reducing CO$_2$: state-initiated measures, private behavorial changes for self-sufficiency, and technological progress. Which is selected depends to some extent on individual and social value systems. An overriding issue, however, is whether we can in principle agree to act on the basis of norms and values in order to reduce the impact of climate change and adapt to its effects. Ethical discourse may help to make these norms and values transparent, thus being a tool for social integration and participation.

Traditional ethics offers three lines of argument to justify human actions as good, appropriate and just. *Consequentialism* views actions in light of their consequences (utilitarianism, as a form of consequentialism, expresses this simply in terms of profit and costs). *Rule-based* (or *deontological*) ethics looks at actions in terms of rights and duties, following the Kantian imperative to "act according to principles you would like to see universally imposed." *Virtue ethics* measures actions in accordance with the innate moral virtues of the human being.

For reasons of brevity, each of the following descriptions of possible measures to reduce CO$_2$ highlights a different one of these ethical systems in relation to each of the three measures. This does not mean that the other discursive patterns do not apply; they could be seen as complementary.

Public measures – Why is climate protection a matter for the state?

Rule-based (deontological) ethics prescribes that we should reduce the impact of climate change for those most strongly affected. The underlying issue here is the inequality in the social and geographical distribution of costs and burdens resulting from climate change. Distributive justice is often the dominant discursive framework in which political measures to alleviate climate changes are generally discussed.[1]

But this perspective is not likely to motivate many people to take action, or to urge their governments to demonstrate the political will required for action. The abstract way in which the effects of climate change are perceived suggests that a rule-based approach should be complemented with consequentialist arguments:

"Impersonal harm-related moral dilemmas are based on reflective, cognitive moral processes that prompt consequentialist moral thinking, whereas moral dilemmas associated with personal harm activate automatically emotional processes that lead to deontological reasoning […] human morality does not envision climate change as a deontological moral issue."[2]

Climate change endangers the lives of millions. Fundamental human rights are at issue here: the right to life, physical security, livelihood, and health; and although the consequences may not affect us all equally, they certainly involve us.

Climate politics should aim to protect us from the damaging effects of these changes. By defining climate rights as an aspect of human rights,[3] they would be linked more effectively to political action for climate protection and sustainability. Complementarily, Grasso argues that we must first tackle the negative consequences of climate change before we can address the issue of justly distributing the CO$_2$ budget.

EXAMPLE — Swiss CO_2 incentive tax

How high should the Swiss CO_2 tax (a tax levied per ton of fossil energy resources) be in order to create an incentive for industry and private households to meet the criteria of the Paris Climate Agreement – namely to reduce greenhouse gas emissions by 30% by 2030?

Accounting to the suggestions in the report of the "Klima-Allianz Schweiz", the tax should be raised to CHF 240/ton CO_2 = c. CHF 60 per 100 liters of heating oil, by 2030.[4]

The tax may create an incentive for houseowners to invest in low-energy houses and/or renewable energies for domestic consumption, but in the rented accommodation market landlords with older properties could pass the tax on to their tenants. Methods of obligating landlords to invest in climate protection without disadvantaging and harming the rights of their tenants need to be developed.

Implementing measures that apply distributive justice is proving difficult on both national and international levels. The question is: Who has to save how much CO_2 to meet the agreed levels of Paris 2015? Greaker et al. (2012) have outlined some relevant principles for the distribution of the CO_2 budget (see below). For them, the principle of equality would allow China and India to increase their CO_2 until 2050. In this scenario the obligations of those two countries are mitigated, while the rights of the world population to avoidance of climate catastrophe are in the meantime confined. According to the principle of sovereignty, however, China's CO_2 emissions in 2050 should be a great deal lower than those of the USA, whose obligations would in this scenario be lessened. In neither case are rights and duties, profits and costs, equally distributed.

Principle	Description
Sovereignty of national states	Proportional reduction of CO_2 budget based on historical levels
Equality of national states	Proportional distribution of CO_2 budgets based on population
Ability to pay	Costs of CO_2 reduction measures to be proportional to GDP
Comparability of payments	Equal distribution of CO_2 reduction costs
Historical responsibility	High historical emissions to be reflected in higher proportional costs in relation to GDP

The issue of ethical distribution of the burden of CO_2 reduction is a good point at which to begin a discussion of national and international options for political action. The scenarios sketched out above may be useful in this respect. Relevant questions are:

- What are the implications of these options?
- What moral issues are at stake in each option?
- What conflicts are possible or likely?
- What level of public acceptance do the various options enjoy?

Private measures: Behavioral changes, individual and collective self-sufficiency

Our individual behavior and lifestyle will determine whether we achieve the 2°C climate goal. Awareness of individual responsibility stimulates decisions about self-sufficiency that involve, for example, consumption and mobility.

EXAMPLE — Individual mobility and air travel

"Commuting and leisure travel together generate a quarter of total Swiss CO_2 emissions. The impact of mobility on the environment depends on distances traveled and choice of means of transportation. Walking and cycling produce ten times less greenhouse gas emissions than traveling by car. So use an automobile (on your own) less, and a bicycle, train or car sharing more …

Air travel is the planet's fastest growing source of CO_2. A single person traveling by air produces in a few hours as much CO_2 as they would in several years' car travel. So travel consciously, and fly – whether for business or privately – as little as necessary. For short trips take the train. Take fewer but longer vacations: flying on repeated weekend sightseeing trips causes more damage to the atmosphere than a single long trip every few years."[5]

Such decisions are often rooted in the human moral characteristics we collectively call "virtue" – the source of the judgments of good and bad on which actions ought be based. A growing body of research from the cognitive sciences indicates that in our moral decisions and behavior we have recourse to both reflective/logical and emotional/affective processes and habits, and that these may either complement or oppose each other.[6] A social dialogue about virtue ethics should address the issue of the conflict between these cognitive-emotional systems.

What Hardin (1968) called the "tragedy of the commons" (i.e., of any collectively held resource) can be remedied by granting social responsibility priority over individual responsibility. This involves creating collective visions and images that foster collective values, rights and actions.[7]

EXAMPLE — Sharing

The "sharing economy" is seen as an important step toward self-sufficiency – and hence, too, climate protection. Sharing an automobile with others instead of having one's own means being mobile and at the same time saving resources. How can we achieve a social environment that encourages sharing? Care must be taken, however, that the "sharing economy" does not have the opposite effect: that an ever cheaper and more abundant supply of goods and services does not stimulate increased demand. For example "ride sharing": in itself this saves CO_2 but its universal availability via the Internet may boost individual car travel to the detriment of more sustainable public transportation.[8]

So sharing must also fulfill certain framing conditions if it is to be socially and environmentally advantageous. Saving resources, widening access to goods, work and services, and increasing social contacts is one thing, proliferating consumption is another – it is a matter of balance.

The two examples above can be used to launch public dialogue and in-depth discussion. Relevant questions are:

- Can individual and collective self-sufficiency help mitigate the effects of climate change?
- What "virtues" must we cultivate to underpin our individual and collective actions?
- What conflicts might arise from individual (affective) actions?

Reducing CO_2 emissions through technological progress
Enhanced efficiency, coupled with tapping renewable energy sources will, it is hoped, enable technological developments to reduce CO_2 emissions to a minimum. Political steps must be taken, in accordance with existing market principles, to enable the global diffusion and acceptance of these new CleanTech systems. These steps include investment in R&D, the fostering of knowledge exchange, and the lowering of trade barriers for clean and efficient technologies.[9]

However, technological progress that optimizes efficiency without lowering consumption will only succeed in postponing the crisis. Schuhmacher (1973) formulated the dilemma of fossil fuel exhaustion long before climate change had entered anyone's mind as an actual consequence of excessive use of coal and oil:

"The illusion of unlimited powers, nourished by astonishing scientific and technological achievements, has produced the concurrent illusion of having solved the problem of production. The latter illusion is based on the failure to distinguish between income and capital where this distinction matters most. Every economist and businessman is familiar with the distinction, and applies it conscientiously and with considerable subtlety to all economic affairs, except where it really matters: namely, the irreplaceable capital which man has not made, but simply found, and without which he can do nothing […] the capital which today helps us to produce – a large fund of scientific, technological, and other knowledge; an elaborate physical infrastructure, innumerable types of sophisticated capital equipment, etc. – but all this is but a small part of the total capital we are using. […] This larger part is now being used up at an alarming rate."[10]

EXAMPLE — The bioeconomy
The replacement of fossil energy sources with biomass can significantly reduce CO_2 emissions. But conflicts arise around the use of available agricultural area to grow energy instead of food, or the intensive dedication of uncultivated land or forest to the same purpose, to the detriment of biodiversity and ecological systems.

According to a report of the EU's Standing Committee on Agricultural Research in 2011, the bioeconomy uses an estimated 2% of global biomass production for the generation of energy. But demand is rising: already in 2011 demand (12.14 billion tons) exceeded supply (11.39 billion tons). In coming decades this will predictably lead to growing conflict for food and drinking water.[11]

Such conflicts must be democratically negotiated among social groups, whether majorities or minorities. As well as cost-benefit analyses, negotiation will involve an ethical discourse about the rights and duties of the various stakeholders.

The logic behind the use of new technologies is largely utilitarian. It is based on the premise that complete transparency about the costs and benefits of human actions is possible. An action is justified if it brings "the greatest good to the greatest number" or if it maximizes benefits while keeping costs and damage to a minimum.

However, this approach offers no solution to problems that derive from the "tragedy of the commons." The depletion of natural resources arises because in a globalized society the individual neither bears the full cost nor enjoys the full benefit of goods held in common, and hence tends to focus his or her actions on the short-term cost-benefit ratio.[12] And this is also true at the level of nation-states: a single country is very likely too small to substantially alter the availability of global resources on its own.[13]

The question of how best to use scarce goods and resources cannot be divorced from the underlying conflict of interests between those involved. The only way to effect an equitable distribution is to take account of the rights and duties of all parties, especially minorities.[14] This means complementing a utilitarian perspective with deontological principles and virtue ethics. In this context Greaker et al (2012), for example, foreground a Kantian ethic which prescribes that each nation-state should act as if a binding global agreement on climate change were in place.

Ethical discussion of this issue might begin with the following questions:

- How can we morally judge the short- and long-term costs and consequences of increasing energy demands?
- How can we transcend short-term decisions of unsustainable energy use?

The foregoing presentation of three current measures for the reduction of CO_2 has outlined some of the underlying norms, values, and moral perspectives that can be applied to the justification of actions, as good, right and just – whether individual or collective. The *Climate Garden 2085* offered the opportunity for interaction and in-depth discussion of these issues – an encounter that in our opinion is an essential element of public engagement. Only in this way can we can understand the values, needs, and expectations of our societies, and stimulate future research.

Notes

1 Barry et al., 2013.
2 Grasso 2013, as cited in Barry et al., 2013, p. 365.
3 Brandstedt and Bergman, 2013.
4 Klima-Allianz Schweiz, 2016, p. 2.
5 Stiftung Mercator Schweiz, 2012.
6 See bibliography in Grasso, 2013.
7 Levin, 2006.
8 Beckmann, 2016.
9 IPCC, 2014.
10 Schuhmacher, 1974, p. 11.
11 SCAR, 2011.
12 Levin, 2006.
13 Brandstedt and Bergman, 2013.
14 Ulrich, 1997.

References

Barry, J, Mol, APJ, and Zito, AR, "Climate change ethics, rights, and policies: an introduction," in *Environmental Politics*, vol. 22, 2013, pp. 361–376.

Beckmann, J, "Wie die Sharing Economy den Verkehr entfesselt," in *forum raumentwicklung*, vol. 02, 2016, pp. 8–9.

Brandstedt, E, and Bergman, AK, "Climate rights: feasible or not?" in *Environmental Politics*, vol. 22, 2013, pp. 394–409.

European Commission – Standing Committee on Agricultural Research (SCAR), "Sustainable food consumption and production in a resource-constrained world," *3rd SCAR Foresight Exercise*, 2011.

Grasso, M, "Climate ethics: with a little help from moral cognitive neuroscience," in *Environmental Politics*, vol. 22, 2013, pp. 377–393.

Greaker, M, Stocknes, PE, Alfsen, KH, and Ericson, T, "A Kantian approach to sustainable development indicators for climate change," in *Statistics Norway Discussion Papers* No. 718, 2012.

Hardin, G, "The Tragedy of the Commons," in *Science*, vol. 162, issue 3859, 1968, pp. 1243–1248.

IPCC, "Climate Change 2014: Synthesis Report," in *Fifth Assessment Report of the Intergovernmental Panel on Climate Change*, 2014.

Klima-Allianz Schweiz, *Klima-Masterplan Schweiz*, 2016.

Levin, SA, "Unity from division: in search of a collective kokoro," in *In Quest of Kokoro/Human Minds for the Planet*, Kyoto International Culture Forum, Kyoto University, 2006.

Schumacher, EF, *Small is beautiful. A study of economics as if people mattered*, London: Blond & Briggs, 1973.

Ulrich, P, *Integrative Wirtschaftsethik. Grundlagen einer lebensdienlichen Ökonomie*, Bern: Haupt Verlag, 1997.

Stiftung Mercator Schweiz, 6 *Tipps für klimafreundliches Verhalten im Alltag*, 2012.

Hothouse stories: Reading the Climate Garden 2085

Caroline Wiedmer

Caroline Wiedmer is professor of comparative literary and cultural studies at Franklin University Switzerland. She has published widely on issues of gender, higher education, law and culture, trauma and memory, and migration.

Stories, it turns out, are tricky. And so is human perception. Stories can help us frame, organize, and understand the world around us, even as they produce blind spots in their quest for coherence, aesthetics, power, and attention. One palpable example for this contest of stories is the current wrangling over whose stories get to determine the lives of millions across the globe, both during the 2016 election season in the US and now, under a brand-new administration. Stories are also crucial in producing and transmitting knowledge, and they are pleasurable in the way they offer both drama and mastery of the world, even as the world itself sways under the impact of phenomena that are hard to grasp in narrative form.

Climate change is one such phenomenon. It is these contradictions between forms of storytelling, reception, action, and catastrophe that I want to think about in this essay on *Climate Garden 2085*, an installation at the Old Botanical Garden in Zurich created by artist-scientist Juanita Schläpfer-Miller and the Zurich-Basel Plant Science Center in the summer of 2016. I want to do so by examining these tensions based on recent works by two cultural critics – Amitav Ghosh, in *The Great Derangement: Climate Change and the Unthinkable* (2016), and Robert Nixon, in *Slow Violence and the Environmentalism of the Poor* (2011) – both of whom take as their starting point the fact that, against overwhelming scientific evidence, humankind seems to be stymied in its attempts to marshal an effective, collective, and timely response to the urgency of climate change. Is it the complexity of the scientific narrative that keeps people from acting? Is it the gaps between perception, knowledge, understanding, and action? Is it a lack of imagination? Or have we lost our ability to read deeply and to be galvanized into action by stories in this (allegedly) "post-factual" world of ours? My attention, then, lies foremost on emerging modes of storytelling and readership, as artists such as Schläpfer-Miller grapple with new forms of narration that bring climate change to life for contemporary readers.

I visited *Climate Garden 2085* very late in the 2016 season, during one of the last events planned to coincide with the exhibition, one that involved a performance by dancers and a sampling of craft beer. At first glance, the exhibition seemed to consist of a collection of plants in two little rows in twin greenhouses. Studying the plaques attached to each greenhouse, I learned that the plants in one had been subjected to a 2°C temperature increase, in the other to a 4°C temperature increase, and that the plants in one of the rows in each hut received 30% more water than in the other. The whole ensemble, I read in the brochure that accompanied the installation, demonstrated what a Swiss garden, with plants typically grown in Switzerland (such as maize, wheat, chard, and sunflowers), might look like in two possible IPCC climate scenarios of the year 2085, which controlled for both temperature and water. In narrative terms, then, many of the usual suspects were in place: we had a setting – the summer of 2085; and a point of view – today's science modeling future scenarios. We also had a theme – climate change; and a plot – a rise of temperature with a concomitant decrease of water; and we had characters – the plants, some of which had performed to my expectations: the smaller, scrawnier ones withered up in the hotter hut, in the row with less water. So why was I – the putative audience for this narrative – feeling so illiterate as I walked through the installation? What was I missing?

I first turn to Amitav Ghosh, a celebrated writer-cum-literary critic, for answers to help me understand why I felt stumped. In his recent work *The Great Derangement*, Ghosh writes on the failure of the novel to impart knowledge about the climate crisis, noting that only very few contemporary works of what he calls serious fiction (by which he means primarily novels that are not of the science fiction variety) deal with the phenomenon of climate change. Ghosh understands our seeming inability to deal collectively with the events that comprise the Anthropocene as more than simply a basic failure to grasp the scientific complexities that surround climate change. Rather, he sees them as a result of the very practices and assumptions that guide the arts and humanities today. "Indeed," he writes, "this is perhaps the most important question ever to confront culture in the broadest sense – for let us make no mistake: the climate crisis is also a crisis of culture, and thus of the imagination."[1] Desire, to his mind, lies at the heart of this crisis; desire – for freedom, for status, for a self as designed and promoted by marketing experts – that has been nurtured not only by novels and poems over the last three centuries, but by a complex matrix of cultural expressions, such as architecture, poetry, and art that was "drawn into modes of concealment that prevented people from recognizing the realities of their plight"[2] and has thus become complicit in avoiding the central question urgently in need of attention: How do we collectively stem the disaster rapidly encroaching on our planet today? What, Ghosh muses, will inhabitants of an altered world think when they search the literatures of our time in vain for portents of the climate disaster they have inherited? How did we, who believe so firmly in our abilities of self-awareness, fail to recognize the calamitous changes that had been staring us in the face?[3] The answers Ghosh offers as to why only a few contemporary writers have taken up this all-consuming issue lie in the intertwined histories of science and literature, and in the kind of writers and readers and literary forms they have shaped over the last two centuries. It is not only the blind desires fueled by contemporary capitalism and consumerism that have brought us to this impasse; the formation of empire and industrialization, he believes, have suppressed older forms of storytelling such as the epic – and with it potentially useful ways of understanding and framing our reality – and thus rendered us incapable of adequately responding to the phenomenon of the Anthropocene. For at the same time as colonization overvalued Western concepts of modernity, it cast humankind not as a partner to "uncanny nature," but squarely as its master. This mastery in turn required an ordered everyday as a background against which individual quest stories could play themselves out – this in contrast to fantastical early modes of storytelling, such as the fairytale or epic. "Thus was the novel midwifed into existence around the world, through the banishing of the improbable and the insertion of the everyday," writes Ghosh.[4]

The focus of the modern novel, in the meantime, was the individual protagonist with his or her daily struggles in a world that was by and large ordered and far away from sudden reversals – a focus that moved the reader ever farther away from communal concerns, as it concentrated more and more on the individual quest. As the Zeitgeist accommodated the narrative expectations which the modern novel held out to its readers, politics too was infected; both turned into just "a search for personal authenticity, a journey of self-discovery." The contemporary reader of literature, but also of politics, became blind to the plights of the collective, or indeed of the nonhuman. Asked by journalist Kay Friese, in an interview following the publication of his book, about the crisis of fiction, Ghosh readily admits that the real issue with climate change is that it is not clear how to shape narrative around it. "It's defying narrative," he writes.[5] In terms of the failure of readership, then, Ghosh's diagnosis is two-fold: there are no traditional narratives that can capture climate change, and even if there were, the contemporary reader, attuned to the demands of the modern novel, can see neither the plight of the collective nor of the non-human.

The story the *Climate Garden 2085* tells does not fail in the ways Ghosh outlines for the modern novel: nature takes center stage in this telling, and the inferred power relationship between human and nature is flipped from that in the modern novel. In the four proposed climate scenarios (2°C or 4°C warmer with 30% more or less water), humans will be well advised to adjust as quickly and thoughtfully as possible to the needs of nature in order to survive. And it is the survival of the collective, not the individual, that dominates this story: the quest narrative of the 19th-century novel is replaced by a quest narrative of the collective. And while there are no ordering patterns that provide the 19th-century novel with the backdrop against which a personal quest can unfold, the *Climate Garden 2085* contains a world of possible reversals exemplified by the plants' relative wellbeing in hotter or less hot temperatures, with more or less water: the last thing this story can be accused of is concealment, or of playing along with – or stoking – desires that in turn stoke the needs of free-market consumerism. What the *Climate Garden 2085* offers, in other words, is an entirely new form of storytelling that avoids the traps which make the modern-day novel unsuitable to tell the story of climate change. But does this also mean, as I initially suggested, that a new mode of reading is needed to receive that story?

To understand this a bit better, I turn to Rob Nixon and his recent book *Slow Violence*. Nixon also proposes blindness as one of the main reasons for the inability to perceive what is happening around us. However, his reasoning is somewhat different from Ghosh's. The main problem, to Nixon's mind, is not so much that authors don't know how to tell the story of climate change, nor is it the ossified expectations the modern novel has bequeathed us as readers, but rather our inability, or unwillingness, as readers to see what he calls slow violence. He defines slow violence as a violence that "occurs gradually and out of sight, a violence of delayed destruction that is dispersed across time and space, an attritional violence that is typically not viewed as violence at all."[6] The examples he gives for slow violence – toxic drift, climate change, radioactive aftermaths of war and nuclear disasters, acidifying oceans, deforestation – are neither spectacular nor easily represented in readily accessible media. For those of us weaned on a digital spectacle of earthquakes, bombings, and erupting volcanoes, sniper attacks, tsunamis, and bombed-out cities, such events of slow violence, Nixon suggests, remain all but invisible. He therefore calls for a re-thinking of our representational strategies, and asks how we can "turn the long emergencies of slow violence into stories dramatic enough to rouse public sentiment and warrant political intervention."[7]

While Ghosh writes about his unease regarding the absence from the scene of novelists who produce stories of climate crisis, himself included, Nixon uses a broader category of imaginative writing engaged in political non-fiction, and turns more hopefully to the many environmental writers who have delved into the margins where invisible misery meets activism, to draw attention to causes that threaten to be diffused over time and space, and ultimately lost to perception and memory. Nixon pays special attention to writers who themselves are affected by the contradictions of representational authority and displacement and who therefore feel "economically, professionally and psychologically unsheltered by precedence [sic]."[8] Not surprisingly, these authors are a far cry from the kind of writers who created the modern novel – often well-situated, mostly white, and usually men of the bourgeoisie who were not writing to save themselves from the ramifications of poverty, race, gender and class, even if they too were often seen as marginalized figures in their own contexts. We readers as well have changed, as Nixon and many others have pointed out. At a time when we are required to look closely, thoughtfully and analytically at processes that are diffuse and often hidden from view, modern technology with the insistence of its flashing images, hot screens, and fast information cultures has utterly transformed our modes of perceiving, understanding, and, finally, reading. Moreover, the particular elements we focus on while reading must surely be influenced not only by our peculiar subjectivities – built by what Nixon calls our Age of Distraction – but also by the urgency with which our very lives are threatened by our attention elsewhere.[9]

Rather than participating in flashy visions of disasters served up for easy consumption – the kind of fast violence we are, according to Nixon, used to consuming on a daily basis – the *Climate Garden 2085* pulls us into a contemplative realm with clear parameters and a multitude of possible perspectives. In part this effect has to do with the fact that it is an immersive, spatial narrative – a narrative that commands not merely our attention, but our very physical being to understand it. For in contrast to the kinds of traditional ink-on-paper narratives both Ghosh and Nixon have in mind, the story of the *Climate Garden 2085* compels us to leave the page by adding sensory elements like sight and sound, touch and smell, and movement. And when it invites us to wander around in the story as though we were on a stage, becoming part of the installation's dramatis personae, it simultaneously asks us to determine our own plot as we walk through the story, and to have our own experience of climate change. The slow violence Nixon claims to be invisible because it disappears over the expanse of time and space, is condensed here by the time-lapse effect of simulated climate conditions that span nearly seventy years and four scenarios. In short, the installation grabs us by our senses, offers us the chance to shape our own narrative, forces us to pay close attention to the inhuman, and fronts the collective over the individual. Most importantly perhaps, it asks us to take responsibility for how this particular story ends.

This brings me back to my own predicament as I stood in front of the two greenhouses on that lovely summer evening in Zurich. Was my initial inability to perceive the tale laid out before me due to a habit of mind shaped by decades of reading novels? Did I yearn for the pleasure of a quest narrative? Was I shying away from the slow violence spread before me? Or had my thinking been compromised by the constant influx of indiscriminate data? Probably a little of each. As a reader steeped in the niceties and predictabilities of traditional narratives, I was expecting a story that I had already to some extent filled with meaning, one that was pre-structured so that the tale of the climate garden could simply be clicked into place like a piece of Lego. I was, in other words, struggling with being a lazy reader indulging in a habit of mind which today might be as dangerous as climate change itself.

For as we wandered around the beautiful Old Botanical Garden in Zurich, a well-known narrative trope was being shaped overseas. During the long fall that marked the 2016 election season in the US, and even more so the first months of the new administration, we have been able to see how a maverick who played on the narrative expectations of millions with his tales of good and bad is now dictating a narrative in which dissenting voices are silenced and the climate crisis has been written out of the story. This example shows us that falling back on old reading habits and comfortable stories won't do. Being a lazy reader has its consequences for politics, for the environment and, ultimately, for the fate of humankind. One way to counter these threats is to create the kind of immersive stories presented with the *Climate Garden 2085* and to become the kind of engaged reader who works hard to assimilate contradictory messages and multiple perspectives, and to take pleasure in discerning facts from fictions. Stories like the one told by *Climate Garden 2085* are a good place to start.

Notes

1 Ghosh, 2016, p. 9.
2 Ibid. p. 10.
3 Ibid. p. 11.
4 Ibid. p. 17.
5 Cf. Baviskar, 2016.
6 Nixon, 2011, p. 2.
7 Ibid. p. 3.
8 Ibid. p. 26.
9 Ibid. p. 277.

References

Baviskar, A, "Civilisation and Madness," in *India Today*, July 21, 2016.

Ghosh, A, *The Great Derangement: Climate Change and the Unthinkable*, Chicago: University of Chicago Press, 2016.

Nixon, R, *Slow Violence and the Environmentalism of the Poor*, Boston: Harvard University Press, 2011.

Nature in the city: Do-It-Yourself!

Christoph Küffer

Christoph Küffer is professor of urban ecology at the Department of Landscape Architecture of the University of Applied Sciences Eastern Switzerland in Rapperswil and senior fellow at ETH Zurich. He studied Environmental Sciences at ETH Zurich, where he also completed his PhD in plant ecology and his habilitation in plant and global change ecology. He is co-chair of the Environmental Humanities Switzerland. His research focuses on urban ecology, biodiversity conservation in novel and human-dominated ecosystems, and global change impacts on island and mountain ecosystems.

Nature in the city is a new trend. Urban biodiversity is an important presupposition for cities seeking a high and sustainable quality of life. The physical and psychological wellbeing of city-dwellers improves with every patch of green, every new species in their environment.[1] And healthy soil with living plants helps cities adapt to climate change. The soil holds water, which is evaporated by plants and trees to cool the air. A rich stock of trees – i.e., many tree species and high genetic diversity – together with intact populations of beneficial organisms protects against the pests that are increasingly threatening urban trees as a result of globalization and climate change. Moreover, many tree species, it is feared, may not survive in the hotter, drier cities of the future. Here, too, healthy soil can help: a tree that grows in good conditions may also survive and even flourish in an imperfect climate.

Cities are refuges for rare species; so much so that they may be able to preserve at least some of the biodiversity that is disappearing ever more rapidly elsewhere. Modern agriculture is highly intensive in its use of land, creating monocultures and spraying herbicides and pesticides so liberally that only a few plants and animals can survive. And nature reserves are too small and isolated for every rare species to find a habitat. Today hope is turning, therefore, to human settlements – and it is a hope backed by statistics. The City of Zurich, for example, contains approximately half the wild plants, mammals, birds, fishes, amphibians, dragonflies, and snails found in Switzerland, and a third of the bats, reptiles, grasshoppers, ants, and butterflies.[2] And, in area, Zurich constitutes only a small fraction (1/450) of the whole country.

We should not, however, harbor illusions. In cities, too, many species fight hard to survive, and many rare species will never settle. The cities alone cannot save Switzerland's biodiversity; but – and this is the point – they can do their bit. Cities can host a wide variety of species: they can be full of birdsong, colorful blossoms, and attractive scents; they are always good for an unexpected encounter with another animal, be it a bird or insect. And the best thing is that – in contrast to nature reserves – we do not always have to "Keep out!" Here we can dig, saw, and hammer to help animals and plants to take root. Nature in the city – Do-it-yourself! No patch is too small to start something, whether balcony, roof patio, courtyard, or backyard, whether neighborhood garden or public space. Simple measures are often all that is needed to create an urban habitat for animals and plants. That is what the first part of this essay is about. The second part deals with a more advanced and ambitious subject: how to attract and support particular species.

Rules for beginners

The beginner should observe three basic principles: a lot of brown, a lot of green, and a little tolerance. Let's look at these in turn.

First, a lot of brown. That means healthy soil, a compost pile, dead wood, and old trees. All these elements provide the nutrition on which biodiversity is based. Soil, compost, and dead wood pulsate with life: with bacteria, fungi, plant roots, and small creatures. In fact there are far more different forms of life in the soil – and that also means in gardens and parks – than in any other segment of the ecosystem. Most of us rarely notice this, but the biological life of the earth under our feet lays the foundation for all the plants and animals that live on and above it. It is this that keeps the soil fertile, so that plants can grow. And, healthy soils, compost piles, dead wood, piles of branches, and old trees host many small forms of life on which larger forms feed; and they also provide many animals – lizards, blindworms, hedgehogs, and birds – with shelter and nesting places.

The first action of the urban naturalist, then, is to uncover sealed areas of ground: to do without, or break open, all the concrete, asphalt, and paved surfaces you can. That is of primary importance. Then you must treat the soil carefully, which is not much work. It simply means not using pesticides, herbicides, or artificial fertilizers, and not digging more than necessary, so that the ecosystem of the soil will not be disturbed. Living creatures dislike being thrown around! These are rules any good urban gardener will follow in any case: promoting soil biodiversity corresponds well with producing tasty vegetables in a garden.

Second, a lot of green. That means having plants grow wherever possible: on the balcony, walls, and roof, in flower beds and tree pits, out of every crack. What sort of plants is not so important, although it's worth taking care that from early spring to late fall enough of them are always in bloom. But that is, in any case, a gardener's pride. A few trees or shrubs create a third spatial dimension of biodiversity, and if they produce fruits for the birds in fall, so much the better. A pond is an attractive extra in every sense; planted with water plants (but better without fishes) this, too, like the soil, will become a breeding ground for the insect larvae on which bigger creatures feed, or for the dragonflies that flit elegantly around town. A patch of grass for playing or lying on in summer does no harm, but leave a corner unmown to provide seed for the birds, and as a habitat for animal life and for the larvae and pupae that cling to twigs and stems of herbs and grasses, waiting for next spring, when they can fly away. For those keen to learn, there are books describing the plant species that are most loved by wild animals; but what is more important is to combine a wide variety of plants, following the practice of every good city gardener. Urban creatures will thrive best in a colorful blossoming paradise.

Third, a little tolerance – a particularly nice rule, as it invites you to do nothing. Not to dig the ground over too often; not to use herbicides, pesticides, and artificial fertilizers; not to weed every corner, seal every crack, mow every blade of grass, repel every visitor with weed-killer. Laissez-faire of this kind need not lead to disorder: the wildness of a city's natural life can be shaped. Off-cuts of trees and bushes can be piled neatly in a corner of the yard; a piece of dead wood can be aesthetically designed or artistically enhanced to make a play frame for kids or a rustic bench for adults – the biological life of the woodpile will not take offense. There will still be plenty of work left, plenty of corners to weed, especially if you have a row of juicy lettuces or a favorite rare plant to cultivate. And, don't forget that the ecologically conscious gardener is never alone: many beneficial creatures can be called upon as allies in the everlasting battle with weeds and pests.

Suggestions for the more ambitious

It is, then, not all that difficult to make a city in a general way more hospitable to animals and plants; but to attract and support particular species is harder. The following section will give some tips and suggestions for more advanced and ambitious urban naturalists.

If you want a particular animal, bird, or plant to settle in your neighborhood, you must make sure the environment provides for all its needs. These include, for example, an adequate nesting place, food for adults and offspring, shelter for sleep and protection from predators, winter quarters, and suitable conditions for mating. Each species has its own needs and its own territorial range in which to satisfy them. A swift will fly for miles in search of food, but a redbreast's territory is less than a couple of acres. All you have to do to attract swifts is to offer a suitable nesting place; they will go out and find their own food, often beyond city limits. But the redbreast depends for all its needs on an area no bigger than a few backyards. The first step toward successful cultivation of a particular species, then, is to make a list of all the elements it needs for its life. Some birds nest in thorny hedges, others in old trees with holes in them. Some feed on the insects in dead wood, others on the blossoms of a specific plant, and yet others search trees and bushes for fruit. Then there are species whose needs change at different stages of life: butterflies, for instance, whose caterpillars eat green leaves, while the adult feeds on nectar from flowers. Many creatures need access to fresh water. Birds need material for nest building, and some need a higher place on which to perch and sing. All these elements must be present in sufficient quantity and at the right time. Food must be available all year round. A few flowering plants with short phases in bloom cannot provide enough food for bees or butterflies. A single wild bee may need more than 1.000 flowers to adequately feed her offspring; a common pipistrelle bat eats up to 3.000 insects a night.

So cultivating a particular species is a challenge. One cannot, in a city, simply rely on the right elements being available in the right quantities somewhere close by. The matter must be approached with pragmatism and modesty. A species that needs a particular plant to feed on will only settle where this plant grows; and that may be impossible in a city. Ambition must adapt to possibility, and the immediate environment is all important: a residential estate on the perimeter of the city can host different species from a downtown block. A location next to woodland or wetland has opportunities that are absent elsewhere. Here you may see frogs in a backyard pond, or a tree-creeper scooting up an old tree trunk in search of bugs.

In these circumstances cooperation is often necessary. A small insect may not need more than a few square meters of living space, and may never leave the same backyard or public park, but larger species will need all the green space available in a neighborhood or urban district. Planning to support measures is, therefore, essential; and this means networking with neighbors and local organizations. There will only be enough nesting (or denning) and feeding places if a group of neighbors pool the resources of their backyards. Cooperation makes ecology into a social project: each district can support and cultivate its own species – and the species will give it a local identity. Wouldn't it be great if Goldfinch Drive had its population of goldfinches, or Frog Walk its frogs?

Plants are in this respect easier than animals: they need the right spot in which to grow, with enough sun (or alternatively shade), and the right soil to feed on – either dry or damp, clayey or loose, low or high in nutrients. If these conditions are fulfilled, appropriate species can be planted or sown – wild flower seeds can be bought in many stores, or gathered on country rambles or while walking the dog. And wild plants – in contrast to vegetables – generally prefer low-nutrient soils.

So don't waste money on fertilizers! Poor soils can host many interesting wild species, and with less natural competition from stronger growths, less weeding will be necessary.

Raising individual wild plants from seed is relatively simple, but establishing a long-term sustainable population is another matter. That needs hundreds of plants of the same species growing and propagating themselves in the same area. If the population is too small, there is a high risk that inbreeding or some external misfortune may result in the extinction of all individual plants of the population. Thus, sustaining plant and animal populations need even more care and forethought than promoting single individuals. If a population is failing, we city-dwellers must support it with new plants or animals. We are like a dating agency, enabling our population to propagate itself in the lonely environment of the city. And to do this we must stay in contact with the urban naturalists of neighboring cities and exchange seeds and young animals with them. That resembles domestic breeding, but in the case of urban 'wild' species we can accept such a paradox. You can grow garden rocket for the lunchtime salad in the same backyard where you breed lizards to liven up the walls – and still keep rabbits there.

So the game of designing nature in and for the city can begin. Where will the nightingales sing? Which community garden will become a habitat for yellow-bellied or midwife toads? Which neighborhood boasts a pair of dormice? Which playground is hosting shrews? How many wild plants will grow on 10 square meters of roof space?

Nature in the city – a basic requirement for the future

It depends on us, what plant and animal species in the future share our cities with us: urban nature is man-made nature. Encouraging biodiversity in the city is worthwhile, not only because some rare or threatened species may find a home there, but above all for our own sake. A rich pattern of flora and fauna is a key factor in sustaining a high human quality of urban life. Plentiful healthy soil and green spaces help cities adapt to climate change. A rich soil life stabilizes water retention in the city's few remaining unsealed surfaces, and this water feeds the trees and plants that transpire the water and thereby cool the increasingly overheated air of cities. The risk of flooding is also lessened if rainwater from ever more frequent torrential downpours stays in the ground rather than running off into overtaxed sewers and ultimately house cellars.

Climate change will, it is feared, threaten many tree species in our overheated, drought-ridden cities. Here, too, healthy soil can help: a tree that grows in good conditions may also survive and even flourish in an imperfect climate. And a high level of biodiversity can also improve other ecological aspects – for example, the health of trees, which in Switzerland suffer every year from the threat of new pests decimating yet another species. This is already a product of globalization and will in future likely be intensified by climate change. The drastic measures sometimes taken against these invasive pests include the felling of whole tree populations. A healthy urban ecosystem can offer a cheaper and more effective solution. Many different tree species with high genetic diversity and intact populations of beneficial creatures can be the best protection against such pests.

Above all, we city-dwellers stand to gain from a rich and diverse urban nature. A good number of scientific studies have demonstrated that our physical and psychological health depends on an environment with enough green spaces, natural sounds, birdsong, and flowering meadows. All the more so if in the future our opportunities for travel are reduced by demands to reduce carbon dioxide emissions to combat climate change. In the sustainable societies of the future, life will increasingly take place in and immediately around the cities where we live. And we will not be happy if those cities contain no natural life, or only its dull remnants.

Notes

1 Lee and Maheswaran, 2011.
2 Ineichen and Ruckstuhl, 2010; di Giulio, 2016.

References

Di Giulio, M, in *Förderung der Biodiversität im Siedlungsgebiet. Gute Beispiele und Erfolgsfaktoren*, Bern: Haupt Verlag, 2016. (An overview of urban biodiversity projects in Switzerland.)

Hauck, TE, and Weisser, WW, *Animal-Aided Design*, Freising: TU Munich, 2015. (A model concept for gardeners and park planners on the promotion of particular wild species. This publication was an important source for the section "Suggestions for the more ambitious.")

Ineichen, S, Klausnitzer, B, and Ruckstuhl, M, *Stadtfauna: 600 Tierarten unserer Städte*, Bern: Haupt Verlag, 2012. (Portraits of typical animal species found in European cities. The following website, which is partly based on this book, gives a useful overview of urban animals: http://stadtwildtiere.ch)

Kueffer, C, "Biodiversität wagen. Neue Ansätze für den Naturschutz im Zeitalter des Anthropozäns," in ILF (ed.), *Landschafts- und Freiraumqualität im urbanen und periurbanen Raum*, Bern: Haupt, 2016, pp. 74–87. (The conceptual background to this essay.)

Kueffer, C, "Nature conservation as landscape architecture," in *ETH Zukunftsblog*, 11.24.2016. (An appeal to understand nature conservation as a design task.)

Kueffer, C, and Kaiser-Bunbury, C, "Reconciling conflicting perspectives for biodiversity conservation in the Anthropocene," in *Frontiers in Ecology and Environment*, vol. 12/2, 2013, pp. 131–137. (An introduction to nature conservation in the Anthropocene.)

Klaus, G, and Gattlen, N, *Natur schaffen. Ein praktischer Ratgeber zur Förderung der Biodiversität in der Schweiz*, Bern: Haupt Verlag, 2016. (An overview of recent biodiversity projects led by communities or private persons in Switzerland)

Lee, ACK, and Maheswaran, R, "The health benefits of urban green spaces: a review of the evidence," in *Journal of Public Health*, vol. 33/2, 2011, pp. 212–222.

Lotzkat, S, *Landflucht der Wildtiere. Wie Wildschwein, Waschbär, Wolf und Co. unsere Städte erobern*, Hamburg: Rowohlt Taschenbuch Verlag, 2016. (An introduction to animal life in European cities, written in a fresh young style.)

Thompson, K, *No Nettles Required: The Reassuring Truth About Wildlife Gardening*, London: Eden Books/Transworld Publishers, 2006. (An attractively written introduction to cultivating biodiversity in backyards and gardens. This publication was an important inspiration for the section "Rules for beginners.")

Urban ecology

Until recently, natural environments untouched by human activity were the undisputed benchmark for ecological research and nature conservation. To see how it worked, nature was investigated in the wild – whether moorland, tundra, or tropical rainforest. The workings of undisturbed nature were the ideal condition to which ecology and nature conservation aspired. This meant, at least in nature reserves, reversing as far as possible the evidence of human impact and re-establishing the original functioning of a purely "natural" nature.

Meanwhile, however, we have become aware that we live in a new epoch: the Anthropocene. Undisturbed nature is an illusion. Human beings and their impacts are everywhere, and mark the ecology of every environment. In the city in particular, human impact predominates, and it is precisely here that ecology has begun to research new models and develop new concepts for understanding anthropogenic nature. Its vision is of ecosystems in which human technology and nature work in close unison: for example, water courses which are partially sustained by artificial pipes and reservoirs but wherever possible allowed to flow freely. Free-flowing city streams, together with good soil in sufficient quantities to sustain the trees that return water to the atmosphere, create a viable water cycle. At the same time, urban gardeners and farmers are looking for new forms of food production that will establish ecological cycles in the city and enhance the fertility of the soil; city planners and landscape architects are designing parks and green spaces to improve the urban climate; and biodiversity specialists are researching how wild animal and plant species can survive in the city, and how they maintain ecosystem services in urban areas. How, for instance, does pollination function in an artificial urban landscape?

This new urban ecology must think holistically to enable a new interplay of many different ecological, social, and technological processes – an interplay that will involve, as a matter of course, interdisciplinary cooperation between scientists, sociologists, and the humanities, and between engineers, planners, and artists. After all, the human being is the most important creature in the city, and the entire spectrum of human needs, values, and activities must be understood and catered for. This means, first and foremost, a will to experiment, incorporating and involving all that dwell in the city: "Nature in the city – do-it-yourself!" means "Nature in the city – find out for yourself!"

An example of current urban ecology research is the project "Maintaining plant biodiversity in cities" conducted jointly by the University of Applied Sciences Eastern Switzerland in Rapperswil (HSR Rapperswil), ETH Zurich, and the City of Zurich's Nature Conservation Unit. Plant ecologists at ETH are investigating the rapid evolutionary processes through which plants adapt to new conditions in the city, and simultaneously using molecular biology tools to determine whether the fragmentation of natural habitats in the urban environment endangers the viability of wild plant populations. City planners at HSR Rapperswil are integrating wild plant habitats into urban open and green space planning, and landscape architects are experimenting with new ways of designing wildflower meadows to meet the aesthetic needs of the city. A citizen science project is drawing residents into this research, with the aim of observing on as broad a base as possible – in backyards, gardens, balconies, roof patios, and flower beds – which plants germinate and grow on their own. The more wild species are already established in the city, the richer will be the shower of seed borne by wind and animals.

This introduction to the new ecological science of the Anthropocene was written by Christoph Küffer.

How to Do-It-Yourself!

How to Do-It-Yourself!

Inside the greenhouses

The experiment was based on IPCC scenarios downscaled specifically for our area (ch2011.ch). The current average monthly temperatures were raised in one greenhouse to represent the so-called 'best case' scenario with emissions controls of at least 50%, and in the other the 'business as usual' scenario, both for 2085. This date was chosen as being within the lifespan of younger visitors. To simplify communication, we described them as +2 and +4°C. The precipitation scenario for 2085 suggests a reduction of 8–28%. We modelled extreme summer drying by giving one row of plants in each greenhouse 30% less water. Air humidity should be 40–60%. Many countries have downscaled the global scenarios for their area, and local scenarios would be the starting point for creating your own climate garden.

The planting method inside the greenhouses was based on some idiosyncrasies of the site; for example, we did not want to dig up the old meadow the greenhouses were installed on, and so an agricultural fleece was laid down and the raised beds placed on top. In addition to the planted crops (see list of plants), we transplanted a forty by one-hundred centimeter section of the flower meadow into each of the four beds in the greenhouses. This was to observe the effect of heat and drought stress on the traditional meadows that are so iconic for Switzerland. These sections could then be compared with the meadow in which the greenhouses themselves were situated.

Outside plot

In order to provide a comparison with current weather patterns, the plot outside was cultivated with the same plants as the greenhouses. The only difference was that we put down a few rows of carrots for the Z'nuni snack box-workshop and added some poppies and flax to brighten the plot up visually.

- **List of plants**
  Wild flower meadow (section cut out of the meadow outside the greenhouses)
  Potato – *Solanum tuberosum*
  Sweetcorn – *Zea mays*
  Rye grass/clover mix – *Lolium perenne/Trifolium*
  Lettuce – *Lactuca sativa*
  Soybean – *Glycine max* (L.) Merr.
  Sunflower – *Helianthus annuus*
  Wheat – *Triticum aestivum*
  Sugar beet – *Beta vulgaris* subsp. *vulgaris* Altissima-group
  Emmer wheat – *Triticum dicoccum*
  Cucumber – *Cucumis sativus*

- **Weed-suppressing membrane**
  www.preisvergleich.ch/tag/unkrautvlies.html

- **Greenhouse**
  https://www.gfp-international.com

- **Solar electricity**
  www.ewz.ch

- **Air conditioner**
  www.kaelte3000.com/web

Steps to take

Choosing greenhouses and plot

We chose a good-quality aluminum-framed, polycarbonate double-walled greenhouse, as we wanted it to last for more than one season. The size you choose is of course based on budget and space, but it is important to calculate enough room for all the plant varieties you have and some standing and headroom for your visitors. With a three by five-meter structure we could create two beds each four by one meter with a one-meter-wide path between them and three by one meters at the front as standing room. The best plot, of course, for a greenhouse is level and sunny, but some afternoon shade does provide essential cooling. It is important that each greenhouse receives the same amount of sun.

Construction

We did not remove the turf, as we wanted to preserve as much of the meadow as possible but we had to cut it out in a couple of places and we leveled the metal base-frame with a simple wood frame made of lengths of seven by seven centimeter posts which we anchored to the ground with thirty centimeter long steel pegs. The foundation is specific to your conditions, but a screw-in post fitting or helical pile is useful for securing the wooden frame to the ground. If you place the greenhouses on concrete, you will have to think about drainage; moreover, concrete acts as a heat sink. Make sure to install all the roof windows for emergency ventilation in case of power failure.

Public access and seating

A wooden deck walkway was laid leading up to the greenhouses and between the beds in order to lead visitors to the entrance and protect both their shoes and the meadow. The decking was underlaid with a weed-suppressing membrane. We also created a three and a half meter semi-circular two-tiered seating area with room for about twenty people, for talks and gatherings. This area proved worth the effort and expense, as it provided a welcoming focal point. We used new wood, which was later reused, but recycled wood is ideal if it is not overly rough.

Cooling/heating system

The cooling system was an indoor air conditioner supplied by Kälte3000, which provided both heating and cooling. Although we were lucky enough to have solar electricity courtesy of the local power company, ewz, we tried not to cool too much, in order to conserve energy. An automatic window opener (with an oil cylinder) worked in tandem with the air conditioner. However, it was hard to maintain a steady temperature and the tendency was to overheat. A de-humidifier would be advisable in wetter weather, as the plants on a reduced water regime benefited from the humidity, and were not as drought stressed as intended. You could rent a mobile air conditioner.

Soil, seeding and planting

An agricultural fleece was laid down, and the raised beds were placed on top. The beds were fifty centimeters deep to prevent root stress. A shallower bed could have been used if no more than the top twenty centimeters of soil had been cultivated, but this would have allowed less control of the water supply. The soil was half garden compost and half topsoil. Some seeds were planted directly and some as seedlings. It is important that each type of plant is comparable with the others of it`s type, whether in the warmer or cooler greenhouse or outside. So in all plots the lettuce was sown directly and sunflowers were planted out at the same time in each greenhouse and outside. whether in the warmer or cooler greenhouse or outside.

Care and watering

The plants were watered by hand three days a week and the beds with 30% less water two days a week. Some pest control was used against red spider mites; however the most troublesome pests were the mice that ate our wheat and emmer harvest!

The sunflowers and maize matured quickly and had to be replaced with new seedlings in early summer. The lettuce, of course, also had to be re-sown after it was harvested. The mature plants could be left to show that plants go through their life cycle at an accelerated rate in warmer conditions.

Outside experiment

Crop management in the face of climate change: till versus reduced-till soil preparation

Tilling (plowing) is widespread in agriculture, where the top twenty centimeters of soil is turned over and broken. This aerates the soil and kills weeds that could out-compete the new crop for light and nutrients. On the downside, soil structure is disturbed, soil moisture decreases, input costs are higher as the soil requires supplementary boosting, and there is greater risk of erosion. A remedy might be no-till, where the new crop is seeded directly in the residues of the previous crop; or reduced-till, where the soil is tilled only to a depth of five centimeters, enough to kill weeds. The additional plant residues mitigate soil temperature change and increase soil organic matter content and water holding capacity, while reduced disturbance lowers moisture loss through evaporation.

Reduced-till and no-till may represent a farming adaptation strategy to the higher temperatures and lower rainfall expected with climate change. Faced with high summer temperatures and limited water supply, plants sown in conventional plow conditions are expected to show stronger visible signs of drought stress than those under reduced-till.

Soil scientist Viviana Loaiza from ETH Zurich planted a till versus reduced till experiment, so she sowed a one by two-meter plot with soybean (*Glycine max*) under two different tilling conditions. One was a twenty-centimeter-deep standard till, as practiced in conventional agriculture; the other was a conservation tillage approach with only the top five centimeters tilled and additional plant material added, simulating crop residues after harvesting. Viviana buried temperature and moisture sensors under each set of plants to monitor soil conditions.

Outcomes

The spring was unfortunately too wet for soybeans, and the reduced-till plants did not perform better than the conventional-till, as there was no drought stress. However, this is an interesting and easy experiment to set up and stimulates conversations with visitors about different cultivation methods. We would recommend a plot of around two to three meters square for each treatment, as soybean plants perform better in a block planting.

Events in the garden

Art (tree) trail

If you are from a wooded area of the world, the chances are that you have an emotional and cultural attachment to trees, if not a physical reliance on them. Woodlands are an important part of the Swiss landscape, providing us with food, places to walk and play, a habitat for animals, and timber for construction and fuel. According to current climate scenarios, several species of trees will die because of the drought associated with climate change. For example, the mighty beech trees that cover the slopes of the Uetliberg, the mountain next to Zurich, will start to die out within the next fifty years. What will our local forest look like then? What will take the place of the beech? Oaks are more drought tolerant; or maybe sweet chestnuts will make their home in Canton Zurich as they have done in Tessin. The Old Botanical Garden in the middle of Zurich is filled with mature trees, some of which will be "winners" under climate change, and others "losers." We invited artists, musicians, poets, and dancers to pick a tree from a list provided – either trees that are going to leave us, or going to join us in greater numbers – and to make an artwork about their chosen tree, and install or perform it under the tree during the *Climate Garden 2085* exhibition. The artwork could be a fixed (temporary) installation, which had to be weather resistant, a performance, or an interactive workshop for visitors. There was an open call and projects were chosen by a jury. Botanist Walburga Liebst developed a tour that wove stories around the trees – stories sometimes punctuated by art performances, enabling visitors to engage with botany and aesthetics, climate change, history, and poetry.

Climate loser tree species were
European beech *(Fagus sylvatica)*
Ash *(Fraxinus excelsior)*
Spruce *(Picea abies)*
Scots pine *(Pinus sylvestris)*
Common oak *(Quercus robur)*
Norway maple *(Acer platanoides)*
European white poplar *(Populus alba)*

Climate winners were
Downy oak *(Quercus pubescens)*
Holm oak *(Quercus ilex)*
Flowering ash *(Fraxinus ornus)*
Stone pine *(Pinus pinea)*
Hackberry *(Celtis sinensis)*
Portugal laurel *(Prunus lusitanica)*
Mediterranean cypress *(Cupressus sempervierens)*
Black locust *(Robinia pseudoacacia)*
Kumaon palm *(Trachycarpus takil)*
Sweet chestnut *(Castanea sativa)*

Concept in collaboration with Michael Kessler, Scientific Curator at the Botanical Garden of the University of Zurich.

Unstable balance
Isabel Rohner

The artist balances herself on an extremely unstable metal frame, positioned underneath a massive weeping beech. It is as if she, in her white garments, is on a sacrificial altar; she alone is trying to find balance in a world off kilter. Around her, and hanging from the tree, she has installed clear plastic bags and tubes, connecting herself, as it were, to the life forces of the tree. The artist believes that "climate change will bring changes that we will all have to react to. If we can find a new balance within the changes, this will open up new possibilities and chances."

Premonition of farewell
Regina Simon

In a meditative and almost trancelike performance, the Basel artist Regina Simon drew the growth rings of the 120-year-old European beech *(Fagus sylvatica)* in pencil on a large sheet of drawing paper. She says that the prospect that the beech, the pillar of many Swiss forests, will at some point disappear, is a painful farewell. By drawing the cross section, she finds a way of connecting to the unique fingerprint of the tree. The uneven hand-drawn lines reflect the irregular growth caused by varying climatic conditions: "It is a creative act, which is mechanically simple and traceable in time. It seems to me as if I as the subject, and the chosen structure as the object, merge with each other – there is a mutual influence."

Hide tree at school

Choreography and costumes: Janeth Berrettini
Dancers: Sandra Hauser, Doris Heusser, Clarissa Hurst, Mercé de Rande, Wolfgang Wehner

Inspired by the 2016 centenary of Dada, the visual artist Janeth Berrettini created a performance at the closing event of Climate Garden 2085. It drew on the iconography of dance at Monte Verità as well as of the Dada movement. The performance took place outside on a meadow where the grass was marked with circles indicating imaginary trees. The dancers started to play hide and seek around these non-existent trees, meanwhile the seeker recited a cut-up text as a countdown:

> The way to success
> I, too, have dry periods
> Balabiòtt
> Light pods, air pods
> A thousand ideas a second
> Mary Wigman
> Why do I have these fantasies…?

Collaging dance, signs, and text, the performance created an absurd atmosphere. Referencing the chestnut tree *Castanea sativa* which is designated a 2085 climate winner in northern Switzerland, Berrettini says: "There is no situation where there are particular winners. If a tree has to die and its place is taken by another, the dying is still a drama."

Storytelling for young children
Minitheater Hannibal

One thing that recurred when we were planning the *Climate Garden* was the theme of storytelling, especially storytelling for younger children. We got in touch with *Minitheater Hannibal*, an outfit run by a delightfully eccentric couple who developed a story especially for the *Climate Garden*. Dressed as a flower and a wild boar, the two actors led their young audience through the park on a hunt for butterflies. Along the way they met different creatures, who all had something to say about how the climate used to be (old tortoise), and the problems they were having now (Suzette the bee with her insect hotel). The topic of photosynthesis, water sharing, what plants were still available for food, and interspecies (plant/animal) relations were all raised in a playful and engaging way.

Trailer
Two creatures that couldn't be more different. Yet they are friends and enjoy arguing about the good old days. Or the good new days? Or the bad new days? Or is it all mixed – some good, some bad? It all depends how you look at it, says Wild Walo. But we're not going to tell you who that is – not just yet. What you can know, however, is that *Minitheater Hannibal* has written a clever story telling you all about the *Climate Garden* and what we are doing there. They will lead you through the garden, and through times to come, keeping close to the biological facts – and close to the human heart! A treat for everyone – not just children and herbivores!

www.minitheater-hannibal.ch

you are variations
Christina Della Giustina

This live sonic event was performed as a public rehearsal by Christina, together with Thomas Jeker (double bass), Christian Moser (oud), and René Thie (electronics), three of the core players of the *you are variations* ensemble.

you are variations creates a musical score by interpreting long-term monitoring data taken from the life of trees. This project has arisen from a collaboration with the Swiss Federal Institute for Forest, Snow and Landscape Research WSL, and its Long-term Forest Ecosystem Research Program LWF.

The work consists of translating and arranging scientific measurements of tree activity into musical compositions. The resulting performances are recreations of the tree as a collaborative, sonic live event which draws attention to the complex water cycles and sophisticated energy balance of trees under different, changing climatic conditions. Christina says of her work: "[…] in associating scientific and aesthetic domains, approaches and practices, the artistic research attempts to address the divide between scientific and aesthetic forms of *comprehending trees*, the differentiation between abstract and actual environments, as well as, eventually, the scope and potential of the space between the tree and us."

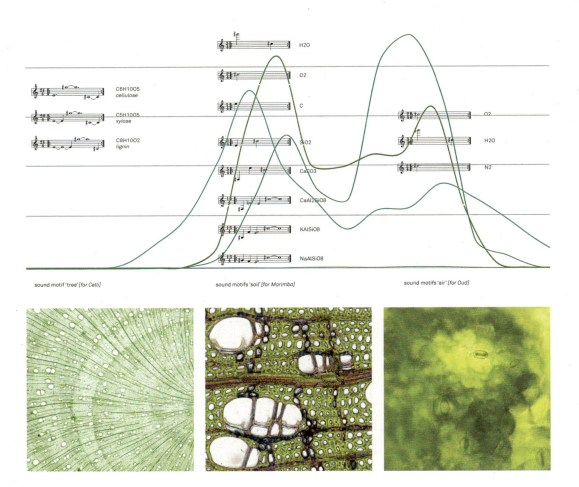

Cypress
Françoise Caraco & Simon Grab

Will we in future stand under cypresses and inhale their aromatic scent without thinking of the murmuring of the sea?

On a stunningly lovely summer evening in July, the artists Françoise Caraco and Simon Grab performed an original sound collage devoted to the cypress in the Old Botanical Garden. A ring of speakers and radios surrounded and mingled with the audience, broadcasting the recorded stories of the cypress, an imaginative journey in time and space, from the Mediterranean to the Swiss landscape of the future.

According to the Persians, the cypress was the first tree in paradise. It is the tree of mourning, of the afterworld and the gods. Brought from Asia to the Mediterranean by the Phoenicians, the cypress featured in the Celtic tree horoscope and was used as a medicinal plant by the Romans. The evergreen family *Cupressaceae* varies in form from dwarfed to high stemmed, from hanging to column, from high-crowned to spreading. The stuff of both myths and classification systems, this tree will, in Switzerland, form part of our future. The audio work invites us to stand under the cypress and breathe in its scent without thinking of the noise of the sea.

To hear the audio work go to: www.klimagarten.ch

Scots pine
Marcus Maeder & Roman Zweifel

What sounds does a thirsty tree make? Do these sounds change over time due to climatic variations? Marcus Maeder and Roman Zweifel aimed to connect sounds that occur in plants with eco-physiological processes and thus make hidden sounds audible. In collaboration with the Swiss Federal Institute for Forest, Snow and Landscape Research WSL, the acoustic emissions in a Scots pine *(Pinus sylvestris)* were recorded with special sensors, and eco-physiological measurement data (e.g., the trunk and branch diameters that change depending on water content, the sap flow rate in the branches, the water present in the soil, air moisture, solar radiation, etc.) were sonified, i.e., translated into sounds. These were used in a video installation with six screens, installed in the Victorian greenhouse in the Old Botanical Garden.

According to Maeder, most of the sounds that occur in a plant arise due to drought stress, including the stress attributable to climate change. The intention of the collaborators was to create an artistic-scientific observation system, providing an all-encompassing experience from very different and complex data sets. The result was a holistic picture of the life processes and environmental conditions of a tree that is under pressure from changing climatic conditions.

For more information
www.wsl.ch/fe/walddynamik/projekte/trees/index_EN
blog.zhdk.ch/marcusmaeder

A video excerpt of the installation
www.domizil.ch/trees.mp4

Treetment – a conversation to be performed
Zoe Tempest & Laura Zachmann

With seven poetic and humorful stories we are led around the garden, visiting seven trees that will be positively or negatively affected by climate change. The artists carry the recordings in a portable speaker, leaving them free to perform a series of movements and gestures in connection with each tree. The text of the voice recordings are reproduced on the following pages.

The texts were spoken by Regula Imboden.

I, Androgynous Flower, am from the family of hemp. Far Eastern in my birth, I seek a park to flaunt my locks. In South Tyrol you'll find my fruit in every homely bake. Come, bite and taste. Evergreen, my downy arms spread out to smooth your cares away. Willingly I'd share my life with you, my City Tree, who are the same size as me: 10–15 meters is just right. Together we'd be ideal for making oars, and fishing rods, and whipstocks.

So if you're interested, get in touch:
Hackberry's the name — one of a hundred species.

03 | Hackberry

Beloved Pine,

from Europe to Siberia I've never left your side. Your family is mine. I love your tolerance toward me and all the dried up soil — the upright way you take upon yourself the warming of the Earth; your endless, creative adaptability. Six hundred years we've been together now, and every day I admire anew your towering frame — full forty-eight meters high. I'd never want to be without you.
But I've begun to worry. I can no longer give you what you need. I'll let you go. I promise, though, the downy oak will never take your place.

I love you. Your Moorland Peat.

04 | Scots pine

Zurich, in the Spring of 2085

At the end of a fulfilled life

European Beech (née Beech)

has, shortly past her 300th birthday, been called by her creator to himself. She loved life below 1000 meters, but persistent drought brought hers to an untimely end. Whoever knew her knows the gap she leaves. Her heart was great, and for hungry pilgrims she kept always a few nuts concealed about her dress.

Mourned by your

native Midlands and all the creatures you harbored.

Since she deeply loved water, her 30 meter coffin will next Sunday be sunk in Zurich Lake. No flowers please. Instead, think kindly of the Beechnut Association. Box 11-2085-0

01 | Beech

May 2085

Take up battle position against the Climate Protectors.
Black Locust, Amazon Queen, show us the way.

On — on to the urban wasteland, we,
the Invaders, are coming
NOW!
With our fertile seed production we will
multiply while the sun shines. Lead us,
Joan of Arc, to our new home!

The spines and blooms outstretched,
we join in combat, reclaiming the city
NOW!
Let the neophytes run wild
NOW!

07 | Black locust

Missing since this morning: a five-leaved acer.
Answers to the name of 'Norway Maple'. Last seen in Europe 2016
in the company of two other soapberries. Of imposing stature, he
is without doubt the most attractive of his fellows.
Norway Maple's distinctive features:
He is twenty to thirty meters tall.
His blooms are both female and male.
His fruits are paired.
His five-fingered leaves are his great pride.
He may hide in damp ravines or on steep cliffs.
Due to a rise in temperature of some four degrees (Celsius),
Norway Maple will likely be fully dehydrated.
In the event of a sighting, gently stop and offer immediate help.

We're grateful for any information you provide.
Your regional Climate Care Department.

Once upon a time there was a Common Spruce, whose common-
ness was such that she thought herself a sphinx. Standing by the
wayside, she let none pass without first setting them a riddle. But
none could solve her puzzle: all were devoured on the spot. The
Spruce grew up, her manners grew worse.
One day a brave man approached upon which, sprucing herself up
to her full height, she brazenly declared: "In the morning it has
four feet, at midday two, and in the evening three. Of all creatures
it alone changes in this way. But when it has most feet, its limbs
possess least strength and speed." Without a thought the man
replied: "You speak of humankind, which in the dawn of life must
crawl on hands and knees, but as it grows, can walk upright on
two strong feet. A third foot comes in age, when bent and weak
it needs support and takes a cane for help."
The Spruce grew pale. She sunk her head and let the stranger
pass. And had the planet Earth not blushed and burned... they
would have lived happily ever after.

02 | Spruce

05 | Acer platanoides

Take your native Ash and expose her to the sun until she dries out.
Uproot and render her to the compost heap.
Bring a Flowering Ash from the Middle East and plant her where
old Ash stood.
Admire her soft bark, her fine prominent blooms.
Call her, on this account, Ornamental Ash.
Beware the fall of her leaves.
Don't forget your native, dehydrated Ash.

06 | Flowering ash

67

Tree (art) trail

Walburga Liebst

The Old Botanical Garden contains not only tree species that may disappear from certain Swiss regions in coming decades, but also other, warmth-loving species that may profit from climate change. Together with Michael Kessler, scientific curator, and Bernhard Hirzel, head gardener of the Botanical Garden of the University of Zurich, botanist Walburga Liebst created a tour of the garden's trees, explaining which might lose and which might gain from climate change.

Swiss woodland is changing. Some trees and bushes introduced for decorative purposes have begun to grow wild and encroach on neighboring woods and forests. Among them are evergreen sclerophyllous (hard-leaved) plants from the temperate and subtropical climate zones of the Far East, like cherry laurel or the Chinese windmill (Chusan) palm. Germ buds of the windmill palm were already found in the woods of Canton Ticino (Southern Switzerland) in the 1930s, but the plant only began to establish itself there thanks to increasingly mild winters from the 1970s onward. Today seedlings have also been found north of the Alps. So the cherry laurel and Chinese windmill palm are among the climate change winners.

Spruce will probably be one of the losers, at least in the Central Swiss Plateau. Natural spruce forests occur in Central Europe almost exclusively in cool, damp regions of the subalpine belt (immediately below the tree line). During the 18th century, a time of cold winters and cool, moist summers, spruce forests spread from there to lower regions. And at the same time human influences began to actively encourage the spread of spruce, which became known as the "staple tree of forestry." Then in the early 20th century temperatures started to rise again. Today they are already in many places 2°C higher than the temperatures in the natural distribution area of spruce. These higher temperatures, and the dryness that accompanies them, lead to drought damage, weaken the trees, and make them prone to invasion by pests like bark beetle. Scientists reckon that in fifty to a hundred years spruce may have disappeared from the Central Plateau altogether.

Scots pine, on the other hand, could be a winner and a loser. This very adaptable tree can grow to a height of thirty-five meters and attain an age of more than five hundred years. As a pioneer plant, it tolerates poor soils, but it needs a lot of light. So in the face of competition from other species it can only establish itself long-term in extreme locations. But excessively dry soils weaken the tree, additionally reducing its ability to compete.

The natural distribution area of Scots pine in Switzerland is the Central Alps, northeastern Switzerland, and the Jura. The species is also still widespread in many parts of the Valais, where, however, it has often lost its natural capacity for rejuvenation, leading to a change in the composition of the woodlands in favor of downy oak. The causes of this change are the biology of the pine and a shift in the usage of the woodlands. Up to the mid-20th century women and children would go into the woods and collect leaves, pine needles, and small branches as bedding for cattle. In addition, thousands of goats foraged there. Both activities were favorable to the forest pine: goats eat leaves rather than pine needles, and the bare forest floor formed an ideal bed for seed germination. Today seedlings are often choked by the thick layer of plant growth and other material covering the forest floor. And in any case a suitable seedbed does not guarantee survival for a young plant. Pine seeds germinate in spring, when the seedlings need an adequate water supply; in prolonged periods of drought at this time of year they will die, despite otherwise favorable conditions for growth.

Pines also occur in Canton Zurich: Scots pine and mountain pine in the Falletsche, decorative pines in Zurich parks, and Scots pine in the Old Botanic Garden, where the gardeners ensure competitors are kept at a distance and the pines can live long and happily.

The Scots pine is featured in the video installation by Marcus Maeder and Roman Zweifel (p. 63), and also in one of the seven beautiful poems by Laura Zachmann and Zoe Tempest (pp. 66–67).

Resources

www.klimagarten.ch

Cinema

The Old Botanical Garden, where the *Climate Garden 2085* was situated in 2016, is the permanent home of the Ethnographic Museum of the University of Zurich. We collaborated with Michèle Dick, a curator from the museum, to screen a series of films telling stories of people, climate change, plants and soils from all over the world.

Thule Tuvalu (2014), the documentary by Matthias von Gunten, is a particularly moving account of two communities on the edge of existence, united by the melting ice of climate change: Thule in Greenland, where the melting ice prevents traditional hunting, and Tuvalu in the Pacific, an island state whose very existence is threatened by rising sea levels. While for us global warming is for the most part a media story, for the people of Thule and Tuvalu it is of existential importance. In powerful images *Thule Tuvalu* depicts the struggle of two communities forced to leave behind the traditional life of their people and face an uncertain future.

Taking Root – The Vision of Wangari Maathai (Lisa Merton and Alan Dater, 2008) tells the story of the Kenyan Nobel prizewinner Wangari Maathai, a woman who made the connection between women's poverty, deforestation, and use of resources in postcolonial Kenya. Organizing women to plant trees for soil protection and firewood, she launched an initiative that grew into the Kenyan Green Belt Movement, a globally acknowledged force for environmental renewal. More than this, however, she ignited a national political movement against poverty, vested economic interests, and governmental corruption. In her role as a national political figure she was instrumental in ending Kenya's twenty-four years of dictatorship.

The Marion Lake Story: Defeating the Mighty Phragmite (2014), directed by Greta Schiller, is a compelling tale of ecological crisis and renewal. An eighteen-acre lake on the east end of Long Island, New York, is being choked to death by an invasive reed (*Phragmites australis*). Marion Lake provides a crucial habitat for migrating birds and rare turtles, and is cherished by locals who remember the beautiful lake of their childhood. The film chronicles the process of activism and ecological renewal of a valuable local resource.

Everything we eat takes its life ultimately from the soil. Drawing on ancient knowledge and cutting-edge science, **Symphony of the Soil** (Deborah Koons Garcia, 2012) is a visual exploration of the substance which sustains life: "By understanding the elaborate relationships and mutuality between soil, water, the atmosphere, plants, and animals, we come to appreciate the complex and dynamic nature of this precious resource." Luckily for us, the narrator of the film, Ignacio Chapela (a microecologist from the University of California at Berkeley), was visiting ETH Zurich; following the film, he and Angelika Hilbeck (an agro-ecologist from ETH Zurich) engaged the audience in a lively discussion about food production and politics.

Citizen science

What is the PhaenoNet?

A long-term project resulting from the *Climate Garden 2085* is a collaboration with PhaenoNet, which enables visitors to observe and collect data on three trees in the garden. This data can be directly uploaded onto a special web platform used in annual reports by MeteoSchweiz.

Observing climate change
The web platform PhaenoNet (www.phaenonet.ch) enables the interested public to participate in the scientific observation of plants. Visitors to the Old Botanical Garden can observe and record the seasonal changes affecting three trees: a beech, a larch, and a hazel. Instructions are given on a placard next to the trees, which includes images from different phenological stages with which to compare the actual tree. The observation can be sent via smartphone and shared on the web platform. Interest in these observations is widespread. These phenological data have proven valuable not only as an indication of the long-term effects of climate change on plants, but also as a basis for climate and weather models.

Plant growth is strongly influenced by air temperature, and this is gradually rising as the global climate warms up. In some species, leaves and buds now appear a good deal earlier in spring: the hazel, for instance, blossoms on average thirteen days earlier than it did sixty years ago.

Climate change can only be demonstrated with long-term measurements and big datasets. Here citizens can help scientists. So the tree data collection project, launched in July 2016 in the Old Botanical Garden in Zurich as part of *Climate Garden 2085*, is a permanent installation.

PhaenoNet is a network of naturalists who share their observations on a common platform. Phenology is concerned with the observation of characteristic phenomena like the various stages of plant growth: when the first leaves or blossoms appear, when the fruit ripens, when the leaves change color and fall. This data is entered in a phenological calendar. PhaenoNet enables school students and interested laypeople, as well as the scientists from MeteoSchweiz, to enter their observations and compare them with others.

Workshops

What does climate change actually mean? What does it do? What does it mean for animals and humans? How do plants cope with it? After all, they can't move, so can they adapt, and if so, how? We developed a number of workshops that address these questions. Through experiments and observations, school students could experience hands-on what climate change means, and learn what greenhouse gases have to do with it, and how we humans are producing greenhouse gases. The workshops were accompanied by an introduction to the concept and aims of the *Climate Garden 2085*.

Gessner prints

Making your own wood-cut prints under the trees was a highlight of the *Climate Garden 2085* summer. Dennis Hansen, an ecologist from the University of Zurich developed a set of exquisite wood cuts from the original animal drawings of Conrad Gessner (1516–1565) and botanical drawings from others of that time. Gessner was a Swiss botanist, zoologist, and physician, and his prolific illustrations of plants and animals are astounding in their detail. But Gessner was of his time, and plants and animals were drawn separately and rarely interacting. Dennis Hansen had the idea to manufacture a set of wood cuts of plants and animals that could be printed on the same sheet; workshop participants could thereby create their own ecosystem of plant-animal interactions. The result was beautiful prints on handmade paper that visitors could take home.

An interesting fact about Gessner is that he was probably one of the first climate researchers: he brought plants down from the Alps to see if they would grow in Zurich.

How many food miles in a Z'nuni snack box?
Apples, pears, cucumbers, and tomatoes are in the supermarkets almost all year round. And they are generally thought to make a good snack. But where do they come from? When do strawberries and apples ripen in Switzerland and neighboring countries? How can long journeys by train, truck, ship, or air make a difference to climate change? It's a question of "food miles." Our exhibition shows both Swiss and tropical crop plants. The workshop is a good opportunity to learn about the different harvest times of domestic fruits and vegetables, and to focus on questions of cultivation and transportation from near and far.

Baskets standing next to the plants contained tokens with the name of the fruit or vegetable children wanted in their *Z'nuni* box (snack box). Their school class could then discuss and evaluate the various choices. On the basis of the new information, children could then revise their choice.

"No thanks, I've got a bag" Plastic bag upcycling – craft activity for all ages
Ah, the ubiquitous plastic bag! Although of course they should, and will, be done away with, in the meantime it makes sense to reuse or upcycle the ones still lying around. We combined several bright ideas we found online, and developed an activity which involved cutting bags into strips and then crocheting them into shopping nets for vegetables. This activity took around four hours and required proficiency in crocheting, or time to learn how to do it. Unfinished projects could be taken away and finished at home.

Solar-wind lights – tinkering activity for children
Using disassembled solar garden lights, we fashioned a mini wind-sculpture that didn't chime but flashed like a firefly when blown by the wind. This activity required simple soldering and wiring knowledge, but we did it successfully with ten to twelve-year olds.

Tree trail scavenger hunt – activity for all ages
Inspired by the Tree (art) trail, the biologist Wendy Gu from the University of Zurich drew a map of the Old Botanical Garden showing the tree climate winners and losers. Groups of visitors of all ages could go on a scavenger hunt through the park and, after locating a tree, bring a leaf, seed, or pine cone back to the start for identification and discussion about why that particular tree might, because of its physical characteristics, be drought resistant, for example. An extension of the activity was to create prints of the leaves by pressing them into quick-drying modeling clay. The scavenger hunt was a very popular activity, particularly on hot days, when the charms of the shady park were irresistible.

Images and resources
www.klimagarten.ch

Help! I'm a stressed-out plant!

The aim was to give an introduction to gas exchange in plants to understand why drought and flooding leads to reduced photosynthesis and therefore reduced food production. Pupils used sensors to measure CO_2 uptake, wet stress, drought, and control in three sets of plants.

This workshop was a shorter version of the "Forecasting the effects of climate change on agricultural crops" and was designed for primary school children.

Forecasting the effects of climate change on agricultural crops

High-school students investigated how stress – e.g., as a result of flooding or drought – affects the uptake of CO_2 in plants. They used sensors to measure CO_2 uptake, wet stress, drought, and control in three sets of plants. A second experiment examined stomata by taking a print with clear nail polish and looking at the imprint under a microscope. A third experiment involved measuring stomatal conductance with a leaf-porometer.

Mykorrhiza – A fungi to fight world hunger?!

High-school students isolated mycorrhizal fungi, stained them, and viewed them through a microscope. Complementing this practical work, students learned at a more theoretical level how mycorrhizal fungi can serve as agricultural fertilizers. Experiments have shown that their use can save up to fifty percent of the fertilizers that would otherwise be necessary. Other research undertaken in this direction with pigeon pea and finger millet (*Eleusine coracana*) was also presented and discussed.

Smart breeding for the future

High-school students experimented with tools used in modern plant breeding. By comparing the genes of different grasses they could identify a molecular marker which enables grasses to resist damaging fungi. The workshop concluded with a discussion with researchers about the relevance of modern methods and technologies in plant breeding which aim to develop crops that are adapted to climate change.

The half-day workshops for high-school students were developed in collaboration with Patrick Faller, a specialist in biology didactics at the MINT Learning Center, ETH Zurich as part of an Agora project funded by the Swiss National Science Foundation. The workshops continue to be offered by the Zurich-Basel Plant Science Center.

Resources

www.klimagarten.ch

Science talks

Reiko Akiyama – University of Zurich
A weed for every weather: Bittercress and their habitat

Lars Dietrich – University of Basel
Thirsty woods: How hard will Swiss forests be hit by climate change?

Cornelia Eisenach – University of Zurich
Sweat, hunger and thirst: Stomata help plants to regulate in a changing environment

Dennis Hansen – University of Zurich
Giant tortoises on the forefront of climate change

Angelika Hilbeck – ETH Zurich
Montezuma's Revenge: Old plants and new technologies

Katie Horgen – University of Zurich
How does your garden grow?
How a changing environment sustains people from Siberia to the Seychelles

Christopher Mikita – ETH Zurich
As above, so below: Soil health in climate change

Melanie Paschke – Zurich-Basel Plant Science Center
Our Garden 2085: The potential of heritage vegetable varieties

Reinhold Stockenhuber – University of Zurich
Could it get a bit warmer?
An alpine plant imagines climate change

Debra Zuppinger – University of Zurich
The potential of biodiversity: Plant species loss and ecosystem performance

Fields, woods, and meadows – and gardens, too – are all affected by climate change. What will our plant world look like in future? What crops will Swiss farmers plant? Which trees will disappear, and which new ones will we see on our hillsides? Plant scientists are concerned with all these questions. The search for solutions continues.

Our evening tours were enlivened by half-hour talks from scientists about their research projects. These were not PowerPoint presentations: the researchers were asked to speak freely and directly to the audience, and there were no limits to the creativity involved! The photo (left side) shows the model of a stoma (leaf pore) made by Cornelia Eisenach from a bicycle inner tube. She used it to demonstrate how the stoma opens when it is warm and closes when it is dry. Both mechanisms are important for the adaptation of plants to climate change.

The lectures reflected the wide spectrum of research dedicated to understanding the impact of climate change on plants, landscapes, and agriculture. In Switzerland, climate change will most probably make itself felt in increasingly frequent heat waves, as well as periods of drought and/or heavy rainfall.[1] This will not only entail serious losses in agricultural production, it will also change our landscapes and affect various ecosystems. The snow line in the Alps will rise by five to seven hundred meters, and the glaciers will melt; this will, in turn, affect water, soil, and air quality. Soils will lose moisture and nutrients and will be more prone to erosion, and this will impact the habitats of many animals and plants. Native species will be displaced by new, warmth-loving species, and the insect world will change in step with these developments. Both agriculture and ecosystems will, therefore, face new, invasive pests in greater numbers. Rising temperatures will, for example, increase the frequency of herbivores in the high alpine grasslands.[2]

Researchers are therefore asking how stable our ecosystems are. Can they compensate the spread of pests and pathogens, invasive species, and diseases caused by climate warming? How – and how quickly – do plants adapt to new habitats and environmental conditions? Reinhold Stockenhuber from the University of Zurich has been examining plant genomes – specifically the genome of Haller's rockcress (*Arabidopsis halleri*), an alpine plant that is common at almost every high altitude. By means of sequencing, he has isolated sections of the plant genome that have changed in the course of adaptation to temperature and rainfall. With this information he can investigate how other species have adapted to climatic variation, and how they are likely to behave in future. That's not all, however: due to the close relation of Haller's rockcress with species like rapeseed, mustard and cabbage, his research may well contribute to the adaptation of crop plants to climate change – for example through appropriate breeding processes.

Again taking a cress (here bittercress) as an example, Reiko Akiyama from the University of Zurich explained how natural crossing has given rise to a new, more resistant species. What is especially interesting in this case is that the parent plants have completely different habitats. Large bittercress (*Cardamine amara*) prefers wetter, less nutritious, well shaded places, whereas mountain bittercress (*Cardamine rivularis*) likes dry, rich, sunny sites. So how did these two species meet? At the beginning of the 20th century, the high alpine valley landscape of the Urner Boden was subject to intense human impact: woods were felled, meadows mown, and ground drained. In the course of these activities the two parent species came into contact, and this has provided their offspring with certain advantages. The new species (*Cardamine insueta*) has an extended (triploid) set of chromosomes that enables it to use whichever parental gene is more suited to its actual environmental conditions.

A major challenge for plants is how to cope with water resources or their lack. Periods of drought like the hot summer of 2015 can cause whole woodland areas to die. Lars Dietrich, a doctoral student at the University of Basel, is researching the detailed background of this mass plant death. Specifically, by measuring the water flow and retention in the tree trunk with sensors, he is investigating how hornbeam, spruce, larch, beech, sessile oak, and Scots pine take up and use water. Every species of tree uses water differently: some wastefully, others less so. Knowing that oak can, as a rule, cope with drought better than spruce, helps forecast how our forests will change in future, and how to prevent the widespread death of trees from drought.

A basic principle in this context is to foster diversity of tree species and woodland structures. A study covering six European countries has shown that biomass production in mixed forests is more constant than in monocultures.[3] In recent years, however, biodiversity has suffered considerable reverses in Switzerland, especially through changes in land use, increasing urban sprawl, and pollution.[4] More than a third of all plant species, and almost half the wild animals, are on the Swiss red list. Many ecosystem functions, like cushioning of climatically induced changes and recovery from them, as well as flood protection, are no longer guaranteed. In her talk, Debra Zuppinger from the University of Zurich emphasized the importance of biodiversity not only for ecosystems but also for agricultural production. "The greater number of species or varieties that co-exist in a garden, meadow, or agricultural field, the more productive the plant community or crop. This is in contrast to the current practice in agriculture and some gardens, in which growing one species or one variety is considered more efficient and productive." Indeed, plants in diverse communities have advantages over plants in communities of one or few species: besides being more productive, plants in diverse communities are better protected from natural enemies and are more stable in a changing environment.

But global warming doesn't just have disadvantages; in fact northern countries stand to gain from it. In Switzerland it should be good for cultivating maize, as well as for winegrowers. So Melanie Paschke, Managing Director of the Zurich-Basel Plant Science Center, encouraged the keen home gardeners among the visitors to grow more winter crops: the newly mild winters we are having make it possible, for instance, to grow chard all year round. Farmers could plant winter crops like winter rapeseed and barley that would also benefit soil structures, as it supports water retention.

The future consequences of climate change depend largely on the quantities of greenhouse gases we emit into the atmosphere, and the temperature increases these cause. Modern intensive agriculture contributes very substantially to these emissions, especially through animal husbandry, which produces large quantities of methane and nitrous oxide. Moreover, the clearing of rainforest – largely in order to gain land for agriculture – is responsible for almost a quarter of humanly caused CO_2 emissions.[5]

Agriculture can, however, also act in the opposite direction, raising the ability of soils to retain carbon dioxide by building up their humus content. Research in this area is currently seeking to optimize cultivation methods. In her experiment, Viviana Loaiza addressed how intensive plowing destroys soil structure and hence reduces ground humidity. This leads in turn to a high risk of erosion. Agricultural costs also rise, as the soil needs more nutrients. The experiment is described in detail on page 46.

Another area of current research interest is in the microorganisms that live in the soil. One gram of soil contains as many microorganisms as there are human beings on Earth, and only five percent of these organisms, many of which are beneficial to crop growth, have so far been researched. Mycorrhizal fungi, for example, support a plant's uptake of water and nutrients, and research has also shown that bacteria in the soil can enhance a plant's resistance to pathogens.[6] Current efforts are seeking ways to apply the benefits of microorganisms more effectively in agriculture.

Plants have a fascinating range of adaptation mechanisms, many of which have not yet been researched. Plant research will contribute to the understanding of how climate change affects the functioning of plants and ecosystems, and how intensively and rapidly it does so. But we must act now. There is a danger that the changes brought about by climate change may be faster than the ability of plants to react and cope with them. We are approaching the limits where adaptation to the global impact of climate change will no longer be possible. Maintaining biodiversity is certainly a keyword in this context: what we plant today will have consequences for the future.

Notes

1 Akademien der Wissenschaften Schweiz, 2016.
2 Pellissier et al., 2013.
3 Jucker et al., 2014.
4 Lachat et al., 2010.
5 ETH-Zukunftsblog, "Methan und Lachgas aus der Landwirtschaft," 2013.
6 Santhanam et al., 2015.

References

Akademien der Wissenschaften Schweiz, "Brennpunkt Klima Schweiz. Grundlagen, Folgen und Perspektiven," *Swiss Academies Reports,* vol. 11 (5), 2016.

Pellissier L, Ndiribe C, Dubuis A, Pradervand JN, Salamin N, Guisan A, and Rasmann S, "Turnover of plant lineages shapes herbivore phylogenetic beta diversity along ecological gradients," in *Ecology Letters,* vol. 16, 2013, pp. 600–608.

Jucker, T, Bouriaud, O, Avakaritei D, and Coomes DA, "Stabilising effects of diversity on aboveground wood production in forest ecosystems: linking patterns and processes," in *Ecology Letters,* vol. 17, 2014, pp. 1560–1569.

Lachat, T, Pauli, D, Gonseth, Y, Klaus, G, Scheidegger, C, Vittoz, P, and Walter, T (eds.) *Wandel der Biodiversität in der Schweiz seit 1990. Ist die Talsohle erreicht?* Zurich, Bristol-Stiftung. Haupt Verlag, Bern, 2010.

Santhanam, R, Luu VT, Weinhold, A, Goldberg, J, Oh, Y, and Baldwin, T, "Native root-associated bacteria rescue a plant from a sudden-wilt disease that emerged during continuous cropping," in *Proceedings of the National Academy of Sciences,* vol. 112, 2015, E5013–E5020.

Walkshop
Humus: soil for food lovers

In conjunction with Sobremesa (www.sobre-mesa.com), a two-hour walk was organized to explore soils and soil concepts in the Old Botanical Garden in Zurich. We looked into the cryptic past of soils for clues toward our future food growing. Soils are complex, sophisticated organizational units not very different from large animals like us: they have a birth, lifespan, and death, and they have a personality and dispositions that make them, like us, more or less prone to certain life strategies.

Ignacio Chapela, professor of microbial ecology at the University of California at Berkeley, asked us to consider the life in soils and query their contribution to what we eat. His talk followed the screening of *Symphony of the Soil,* a film narrated by Chapela, which had been shown earlier the same week.

Evaluation

The *Climate Garden 2085* was well received by visitors. Both high school and primary (grade) school teachers were particularly appreciative "as it made climate change tangible" and many visitors, including high-school students, found the discussion at the end of the guided tour or workshop interesting and informative. This confirms our intended concept to use the garden as a catalyst for discussion. Intimate discussions were made possible by having many small events, where people had time and space to talk to plant scientists, professional guides, or students.

The *Climate Garden 2085* was evaluated on three levels; by monitoring visitor numbers, on-site feedback on individual events, and overall evaluation after the event via online questionnaire.

Monitoring data
A log file of visitor numbers was kept for each individual event, and a weekly tally of visitors to the gardens was kept from April to mid-September. There were a total of 122 events over twenty-five weeks.

Number of participants for each event:

Lunch talks	282
Science talks	122
Storytelling for children	86
Film showings	97
School groups	450
Art and botanical tours	380
Private tours	376
General visitors (not registered for an event)	9045

We were very pleased with the number of communications professionals who visited, and with the number of school groups, both primary and secondary. Overall we achieved our projected visitor numbers. The number of participants in the family workshops was disappointing. This was partly attributable to the weather being too cold and then suddenly too warm. The weather was again not in our favor for the theater events, and we could not change many dates, as the theater players were fully booked throughout the summer.

On-site feedback
Feedback cards were created and laid out in one of the greenhouses, as well as on the seating area when the garden was staffed. They asked simply: How did you like the exhibition? On the bottom of the card was also the link to the online survey. About fifty cards were filled out, the majority of the responses were very positive. Visitors said they particularly enjoyed the discussions at the end of the talks and workshops. When they were referring to a specific workshop, we were able to integrate appropriate feedback.

At the end of the school workshops and public tours there was always time for questions and comments. This dialogue with the visitors gave us a good insight into their opinions on climate change and food production in Switzerland. These opinions were often quite polemical, ranging from climate change doubt to the critique that our greenhouses showed too many "climate winners" among the plants, and that we were too optimistic and "technocratic" in postulating scientific solutions to problems of food production and adaptation to climate change. We were thereafter careful to emphasize that science can contribute to the solutions, but CO_2 emissions reduction also requires political and social action.

Online questionnaire
Using Survey Monkey, we created a nineteen-item questionnaire that took approximately ten minutes to complete. We offered a free copy of our handbook for every completed survey. We received thirty-five completed surveys, and fourteen respondents declared their profession. These included teachers, climate change professionals, social workers, and one artist. This provided useful critical feedback. The questions included a general rating of the project, personal likes and dislikes in the project, what could be improved in the project, what can

be done by the individual to mitigate climate change, and the role of science in society. There was also space for comments to the organizers.

In evaluating the surveys, we focused on feedback that will help the next iteration of the *Climate Garden 2085* and opinions about climate change, science, and society which interest us as an institution.

From the thirty-five responses, the overall satisfaction rate was high: forty-seven percent said the garden was very good or good, and fifty percent fairly good, only one person rated it as not at all good; however, the same person said they liked the basic idea. Some quotes: "The Tree (art) trail was fascinating, especially the climate winners and losers – Juanita Schläpfer-Miller's passion came across well. She conveyed it with great charm – the idea of having two greenhouses for comparison – 'blue' images with the 'photo method' – getting to know the Old Botanical Garden."

Constructive criticism
In answer to the question of what we could improve, there was a desire to see stronger differences between the greenhouses and that they should be bigger, with more plants, and left to run for more years so that one could see the difference over time. It was part of our concept that we had minimal text in the greenhouses, but four respondents thought there should be more text, especially for people who did not take part in a talk or workshop. We also received this feedback from visitors on site in May, and were able to respond by adding more plant signs. However, this was clearly insufficient for some visitors, and it would be advisable to have more information about what visitors should expect to see. This could be done with an audio recording, or a short video tour – good ideas, but unfeasible because of lack of resources.

There were several comments with suggestions about the temperature and humidity. In retrospect we should have made a clear printed statement not only that the greenhouses reflected an average monthly daytime temperature and additional extremely hot days in summer, but also that the temperature sank at night, and that humidity only reduced if the air-conditioning system was cooling. Temperature control and humidity were not as precise as we would have liked, and we would highly recommend that future versions of the garden be positioned in partial shade and use a de-humidifier as well as air-conditioning. It is debatable whether average temperatures are the correct value to use, and how the temperature increase on hot summer days should be integrated (see Fachbericht MeteoSchweiz, vol. 243, 2014: "Klimaszenarien Schweiz – eine regionale Übersicht").

However, despite the greenhouses having limitations as a model, there was considerable positive feedback about the effectiveness of the garden from a didactic point of view. Twenty-nine respondents used the terms "tangibility," "visualization," "demonstrative," or "concrete" as positive attributes. Many said they liked the idea of making climate change experiential: "The idea is very interesting, and making climate change into a real experience is an excellent way of getting it across to as many people as possible. You're doing a great job. Keep at it!"; "I agree with the idea behind the project, and I really like the simplicity of the presentation. But I thought the overall result was a bit thin – possibly because our visit coincided with the end of the plant life period."

This would be something to address in the next version of the garden. Although toward the end of the project the plants had completed their lifecycle and were dried out, they were still comparable with the outside beds. At this point it would have been beneficial for the visitors to have photos of the plants in their earlier stages.

Several comments mentioned the idea of integrating art performances as interesting: "The idea of combining a climate change presentation with art performances appeals to me"; "[…] melding art and science."

Personal attitudes to climate change
To the question "What can you do against climate change?", thirteen answers recommended reducing flights and car use, thirteen reducing meat consumption and buying local seasonal produce, and five reducing consumption in general. Four respondents said they did not learn anything new from the event they attended.

We asked which scientific research themes respondents were concerned with. Examples we gave were:
- Breeding plants that are more resistant, e.g., that consume less water and survive extreme weather events. And, plants that can fight against new diseases and pests.
- Adapt farming methods in agriculture to reduce carbon emissions and minimize greenhouse gas emissions.
- To develop climate models that allow predictions of the consequences of climate change. For example: What effects does a temperature increase of 4°C have on agriculture and forestry, on plant diversity, or on our water reserves.
- Climate-friendly urban development by avoiding the emission of greenhouse gases (climate protection) and measures to adapt to the consequences of climate change (climate adjustment): for example, more green areas and diverse plant species in the city.

A surprising eighty-eight percent said it was less important to do research on climate models than on climate-friendly city development (eighty-one percent "very important"). This may mean that respondents thought that climate models have been sufficiently researched and research applied to city planning is now more urgent.

Fifty-eight percent thought it was important to conduct research on drought-resistant plants as compared with twenty percent who thought research on soil cultivation methods was necessary. It may be that this question was not clear, as a full forty percent checked "I don't know." Asked what are your concerns about climate change, more than eighty-seven percent of respondents are worried by climate change and the keywords here are "climate wars," "water shortages," "migration," "lack of understanding in politics and society."

Summary
- The theme of plants – as food and landscape – and the local impacts of climate change attracted a broad and interested public, from primary school students to managers.
- Visitors found the experiment and presentation novel and experiential.
- We had good critical feedback from communication professionals.
- Many events allowed time and space for dialogue.
- Survey respondents made clear statements about actions they could take to limit their carbon footprint.
- The surveys and feedback at events showed a high visitor-satisfaction rate.
- Overall we achieved our projected visitor numbers.

Recommendations for next time
- More explanation of what visitors should see – perhaps with an audio tour when the exhibition is not staffed.
- A poster or info-graphic showing the climate models (these were only provided for part of the tour), and a clear written explanation of chosen parameters.
- Five or six take-home messages on a poster by the exit, or on cards for people to take with them.
- Use surveys as well as feedback cards as part of the on-site evaluation, rather than just as overall evaluation after the event.
- Either run the exhibition for a shorter time (four months) or provide more explanation of results in the phase when the plants were dying.

Observations of the Climate Garden 2085 experiment

We called the *Climate Garden 2085* a public experiment, as it was designed to provoke discussion rather than produce scientific data. In any exhibition compromises have to be made based on the budget and time frame available. There have been numerous excellent scientific studies on the effects of climate-change-induced drought, flooding, temperature, and elevated CO_2 levels on agricultural crops, alpine plants, and trees. It would have been impossible, and indeed undesirable, for us to attempt to recreate these in our simplified model. However, the deviations from scientific studies became talking points, and we could discuss with visitors the lack of extreme weather events and ecosystem function, and even the fact that by 2085 the current plants will have already somewhat adapted – our model could not take this into consideration. The text here from Olivia Wassmer, one of our *Climate Garden 2085* guides, is a description of her observations of heat and drought stress on the plants we cultivated.

Potato
The potatoes initially showed a marked difference in stalk growth: in the 2°C warmer greenhouse the stalks grew more quickly than outside, and under the 4°C warmer regime growth was even faster, so that the stalks soon had to be held upright, while those outside were still bright green and bushy. If this rapid growth had taken place outside, the stalks would have been blown over by the wind, which would have led to considerable loss of yield.

The ripening process – when the stalks dry out – began earlier in the 4°C warmer than in the 2°C warmer regime, although here, too, the plants again ripened earlier than those outside. The best yield (c. 3 kg.) was from the plants in the 2°C warmer greenhouse with 30% less water. Those watered normally were attacked rather more by late blight, which diminished the yield to 2.5 kg. Both potato beds in the 4°C warmer greenhouse had a similar yield: 2.7 kg. with normal watering and 2.3 kg. with 30% reduced watering. The potatoes outside were affected by heavy rain in the spring; at 2.4 kg. their yield was similar to that of the plants in the 4°C warmer greenhouse.

Sugar beet

A comparison between the sugar beet grown outside with that grown in the 2°C warmer greenhouse showed that the leaves of the greenhouse plants were far smaller and drier. Moreover, the impact of water reduction was clearly visible: the roots of the plants with 30% less water had only half the diameter of those watered normally. A 4°C rise in temperature led to even smaller leaves.

Sugar beet right: 2°C warmer, 30% less water
Sugar beet far right: 2°C warmer, normal watering

Sunflower
Especially at the beginning of the project, the sunflowers showed noticeable differences. The higher temperatures boosted growth, and the watering regime also made a difference: the stems of the plants treated with a normal quantity of water were double the thickness of the others. The first plants were already ripe in May, and new ones were planted. In the second half of the season these were infested by spider mites, which impaired their growth and made comparison difficult.

   Sunflower above: 2°C warmer, 30% less water
   Sunflower below: 2°C warmer, normal watering

Maize
Maize was also positively affected by the higher greenhouse temperatures, and its rapid growth enabled several generations to be harvested, whereas only one generation of the maize planted outside actually ripened.

Meadow
The section of meadow transplanted into the greenhouse did relatively well in both regimes. Differences were observable in the size of the leaves of the various plants, but otherwise neither the composition nor the yield changed significantly. To observe change in this group of plants, the project would have to run for several years.

Wheat
Wheat took a relatively long time to produce a head under all five regimes. In the second half of the season the wheat planted outside had to struggle against wheat leaf rust and had fewer healthy ears. The wheat plants in the 2°C warmer greenhouse looked healthy, but the plants given 30% less water had significantly more brown leaves. The plants in the 4°C warmer greenhouse showed clear signs of stress: with both normal and 30% reduced watering they looked brown and dried out. Their yield was also significantly lower than that of the plants outside and in the other greenhouse: their ears were both smaller and fewer. The emmer in the greenhouses grew very fast at the beginning of the project, but seemed notably unstable in comparison with the plants outside. However, the yield was not measurable, as by fall most of the ears had been eaten by mice.

Lettuce
The lettuce grew considerably faster in both greenhouses than outside, but needed a good deal more water.

Soybean
Soybean grew better in both greenhouses than outside: under the 4°C warmer regime the stalks were almost double the length of those outside, and more fruit ripened.

In conclusion one can say that there were in the *Climate Garden 2085* – and will be in future – winners and losers. Soybean is certainly a winner, as too are sunflowers and maize. Wheat and emmer yields will greatly decrease, and sugar beet will also grow less well as the climate warms. The experiment shows that in all probability different plants will grow in Switzerland in 2085 than those with which we are familiar. We will eat differently, and will have to get used to a different landscape.

Editors

Photographer

Manuela Dahinden, a science communication specialist with a PhD degree in molecular biology, has been Managing Director of the Zurich-Basel Plant Science Center for the past ten years. Manuela's core concern is with science transfer and the public understanding of science – fields in which she has, with the cooperation of scientists active in their particular fields, built up a wide spectrum of offers on topical research issues. These range from specialist conferences, through discussion groups, workshops for school classes and teachers, to family expeditions and science summer camps. Her commitment to the natural sciences stems from simple curiosity about the how and why, and from awareness of the growing importance of knowledge of plants for our lives. She has a passion for design and creationship.

Juanita Schläpfer-Miller is a science communicator and artist. Juanita studied transdisciplinary knowledge production in art and science, and has been actively involved as a science communicator at the Zurich-Basel Plant Science Center for the past five years. With many years' experience in museum design and public engagement with science, her work has ranged from particle physics to climate change. She has a passion for tinkering and organizes workshops for children and youth in which they can experience and research experimentally into both plant life and technology. A global nomad, she has lived, worked, and gardened in Switzerland for twenty years.

Nina Mann is an artist and photographer. As well as freelance work, she is known for her conceptual design and art-in-architecture. She is also a dedicated portrait photographer. Commissioned by the company's art collection, she created a photographic record of the five-year rebuilding project at the landmarked head office of Zurich Cantonal Bank – a task that generated two publications and a limited edition series of art prints. Fifty-nine works from this period are in the bank's art collection, and Nina Mann is also represented in the art collections of the Canton of Zurich and the City of Biel, as well as in many private collections in Switzerland and beyond. Her photographs have been widely shown in both solo and group exhibitions. Born into a Czech photographer family, she has lived and worked for more than thirty years in Switzerland.

Contributors

Dance, performances, sound & video installations
Janeth Berrettini
Francoise Caraco & Simon Grab
Christina Della Guistina
Minitheater Hannibal: Andrea Fischer-Schulthess & Adrian Schulthess
Markus Maeder & Roman Zweifel
Isabel Rohner
Regina Simon
Zoe Tempest & Laura Zachmann

Tours & workshops
Susanne Burri
Lorenz Diefenbach
Wendu Gu
Dennis Hansen
Sabrina Keller
Walburga Liebst
Barbara Roth
Ursula Wegmann
Olivia Wassmer
Regula Zahnd

Sobremesa
Laura Schälchli

Science talks
Reiko Akiyama
Lars Dietrich
Cornelia Eisenach
Dennis Hansen
Angelika Hilbeck
Katie Horgen
Christopher Mikita
Melanie Paschke
Reinhold Stockenhuber
Debra Zuppinger

Gardener
Samuel Burgi

Construction
Beat Schläpfer, www.a-faire.ch
www.zimmerei-oberhaensli.ch

Resources

PDF downloads (in German)
Program brochure
Student workbook on climate change
Student workbook on symbiosis
Student workbook on plantbreeding
Information cards: Z'nuni snack box
Information sheet: What do plant scientists study?
Information sheet: Tree art trail

www.klimagarten.ch

Acknowledgements

The *Climate Garden 2085* was created by the Zurich-Basel Plant ScienceCenter in collaboration with the Botanical Garden and the Ethnographic Museum of the University of Zurich.

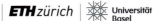

We are grateful for the financial support from
Swiss National Science Foundation
Swiss Federal Office for the Environment
Swiss Federal Office for Agriculture
Foundation Mercator Schweiz
Ernst Göhner Foundation
Biedermann Mantel Foundation
Migros Kulturprozent
Enea Landscape Architects GmbH
Garden Center Hauenstein Rafz
School and Sport Department of the City of Zurich
Swiss Re
Kälte3000
VBZ
ewz

Thank you for technical & creative input
Verein GLOBE Schweiz, Eric Wyss
Environmental Humanities Switzerland
ProClim, Gabrielle Müller
Communications Office of the University of Zurich
Zurich University of the Arts, Irene Hediger
Botanical Garden of the University of Zurich,
    Michael Kessler, Bernhard Hirzel and Peter Enz
Ethnographic Museum of the University of Zurich,
    Mareile Flitsch and team
Meury Architecture GmbH, Ralph Meury